The Black-throated Finch

The Southern Black-throated Finch (Poephila cincta cincta) is one of 12 granivorous birds (one-third of the total) that have declined from the subtropical and tropical savannas across Australia's north.

The Black-throated Finch has lost 80% of its habitat, and is now extinct in New South Wales. Two main population strongholds remain, the Townsville area and the Desert Uplands bioregion which contains the proposed Adani coal mine.

The major threats to the finch are habitat loss and habitat degradation.

Field investigations by Stanley Tang in April 2013 resulted in the discovery of the largest known population of the Black-throated Finch. They were located in the proposed Adani coal mining site. The flock contained 400 birds. Monitoring of flocks confirm that the largest ones are in the Adani mine site, demonstrating that it is the most important habitat remaining.

Stanley Tang recalls his discovery: 'After fruitlessly scouring the harsh country of central Queensland for days in search of the endangered Southern Black-throated Finch, the moment I finally heard its familiar descending whistle was a moment of relief and thrill … the 400-strong flock of birds that subsequently filled the sparse trees took my breath away.'

– Dr April Reside

ADANI
VERSUS
THE
BLACK-THROATED
FINCH

TOR HUNDLOE

Australian Scholarly

Pamphleteer is an Australian Scholarly imprint.

First published 2018 by Australian Scholarly Publishing Pty Ltd
7 Lt Lothian St Nth, North Melbourne, Vic 3051
TEL: 03 9329 6963   FAX: 03 9329 5452
EMAIL: aspic@ozemail.com.au   WEB: scholarly.info

ISBN 978-1-925588-90-3

ISBN 978-1-925588-92-7 (ebook)

Cover design: Wayne Saunders

Contents

Preface

Australian coal mining is about to have its future determined by a battle of wills and economic forces. The idea of a battle of wills we can relate to, as this is nothing more or less than the human energy that transforms itself into political power at the ballot box. The role of economics is more obtuse. While we will pay attention to our quarterly electricity bill, we are unlikely to undertake regular economic modelling of the energy sector. We tend to leave that to the experts – until now that is. Coal burned generates electricity and greenhouse gases. The sun, the wind and falling water also produce electricity – without emitting carbon dioxide. Sooner or later – sooner – the new will outcompete the old on price.

A few words on the battle of wills, in which two sides fight to be heard and their requests recognised by those who make the big decisions that impact on all of us. Big decisions can settle on the survival of a little bird.

On one side of the battle are the very few Australians who have been granted the right to mine and sell coal, their foreign mining partners, a few foreigners without Australian partners, the financial intermediaries who have made and make loans or otherwise have a monetary interest in the profits from mining, the Commonwealth government as a beneficiary through income taxes paid in Australia, and the State governments to whom royalties are paid by those granted the right to the coal. This is an extremely powerful coalition. Both money and the media are its handmaidens.

On the other side are numerous environmental organisations working co-operatively or individually, public interest legal organisations, a small number of progressive think tanks, some farming and rural interest groups, plus a significant number of individual Australians.

A battle of wills follows a battle for 'hearts and minds'. Both sides engage in the process to attract voters. Voters are crucial to the outcome of the battle due to the fact that only governments have the powers to approve or disapprove mining, and voters make or break governments.

It is true that the pro-mining side requires far fewer supporters because it has both strong support from powerful media outlets and deep pockets to run advertisements on television, in newspapers and via the social media. This we witnessed with its opposition to, and defeat of, the proposed mining rent (resource) tax.

However, ethical principles and economic realities have their own imperative and the future need not resemble the past.

The battle over coal mining is vastly different from past Australian environmental campaigns. It is not simply and totally a 'green' issue, such as protecting endangered animals or dealing with the threat of increased greenhouse gas emissions on the health of the Great Barrier Reef. Of course, both of these matters are critically important as there are endangered animal and flora species in the areas sought for mining, and their protection, likely to be through environmental offsets, is but one of the most basic matters to be dealt with if the Adani mine is to be sanctioned. And as the story that unfolds makes abundantly clear, any significant addition to the existing level of carbon dioxide and other greenhouse gases in the atmosphere is a genuine threat to the Great Barrier Reef. Burning coal is a major source of increased carbon dioxide.

It is possible, but by no means guaranteed, that public opinion in favour of the environment will stop the opening of more coal mines. In contrast to the past campaigns to protect unique Australian natural environments – campaigns that were won – the environmentalists, and the voters who have fallen in behind them, face a completely different and more complex task in stopping coal mining. A few preliminary comments on this are warranted.

First, we must not overlook the central role coal plays in the global economy and, because our story is an Australian one, coal's dominant position in earning income for the country. Don't pay much attention to the jobs that are touted to result, as coal mining is very capital intensive and the machinery is more than likely imported. What counts are the royalties and income tax.

It needs to be recognised that mining and selling coal could generate considerable more money for its owners, the Australian citizens, than the amount it does at present. If we are to sell coal regardless of the negative impacts, Australian governments should take seriously their responsibilities to ensure that both royalty and tax arrangements are fair, that is provide money that could be put to good cause for the actual owners of what is underground. Without giving any secrets away, ones that will be exposed later in this book, Australian tax-payers are providing subsidies to coal miners and, hence, selling our coal at give-away coal prices. Is charity owed to coal miners?

The story is no 'Wild West' conflict between white-hatted 'goodies' and black-hatted 'baddies'. If it looks like that some have benefited and others have lost, we need to be careful before coming to judgement. Presented with perverse incentives and conflicting objectives – as we will see is the case with coal mining and environmental goals – various players can act in a manner that is contrary to the common good. This does not have to be deliberate. The failures of processes and of institutions, and a lack of a defining social and economic philosophy, underpin the story as it gradually moves to its conclusion. Yet, there might be a 'black-hatted baddie' to be unveiled.

Once we focus on the role of coal to generate electricity we are obliged to consider a future where alternative sources of energy compete with coal. Competition can and, as history shows, does destroy the 'old' as it is replaced by the 'new'. The writing is on the wall, the evidence on suburban roof-tops and on coastal hills. Household solar panels, wind farms and pumped-hydro electricity generation are replacing coal and the other fossil fuels. The only sensible debate – there are many non-sensible ones – is about the date that the coal age ends. If that is still some decades into the future, those favouring coal mining will have their hand strengthened in the present debate. However, the future for coal is likely to be contingent on successful, and economically feasible, carbon capture and storage, as there is no likelihood that we will be able to offset the release of carbon dioxide from the burning of coal in large-scale power stations. Offsetting the global warming caused by burning coal in mammoth power stations is far removed from the planting of a few trees to compensate for your next flight between Sydney and Melbourne.

Furthermore, if we are to consider the continuation of mining and selling coal – as we must realistically do at least for the short term – we must determine how we use the income that accrues to us, via our governments. The answer, surely, must be the immediate establishment of a sovereign wealth fund. This is the only means by which we can compensate (offset) the depletion of a non-renewable resource.

There is no better candidate to explore the matters outlined here than the story of the Adani coal mine. Adani is a name for the history books. And so might be the future of a small endangered bird, the Black-throated Finch – it is a name to remember.

*The dramatic reduction in the ristribution of the Black-throated
Finch and the site of the proposed Adani mine.
Map by Eric Vanderduys.*

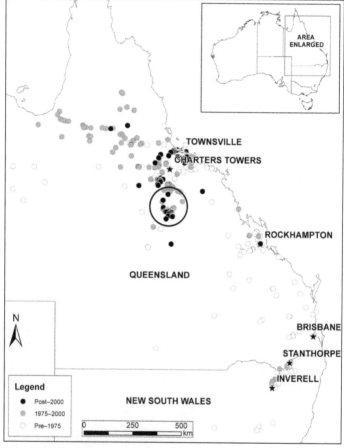

The light dots show the distribution of the finch pre-1975, the
grey dots between 1975 and 2000 and the black dots since 2000.
The circle is the site of the proposed coal mine.

1

Introduction

The proposal to develop the largest coal mine in Australia, in an era of heightened concern about the ever-increasing build-up of greenhouse gases in the atmosphere and the threat that climate change poses for the health of the Great Barrier Reef, guaranteed that controversy and conflict would trump any chance of consensus on the Adani coal mine. This proposed coal mine is destined to become the best-known environmental battle in Australia's history.

The mine commonly called the Adani mine is more formally the Carmichael Coal Mine. The Adani title refers to its proponent, the Adani Group chaired by Mr Adani. As there is a railway line proposed to be built to service the mine, the formal documents refer to the overall project as the 'Carmichael Coal Mine and Rail Project'. The rail line would be a track of some 189 km, linking to an existing rail line going to the Queensland coast, adjacent to the Great Barrier Reef. Extension of port facilities, owned by the same Mr Adani, and the prospect of transporting much more coal (a very large quantity is already exported) through the coral cays and 'bombies' (under-water coral assemblages) of the Great Barrier Reef is opposed by environmentalists. This is a separate story to the one told here.

The casual observer of what is the 'Adani Coal Mine Battle' is likely to interpret it as yet just another environmentalist versus developer contest, of which many have been fought in Australia over the past 50 years. However, the Adani case is very different to previous environmental disputes. This will become clear as the story evolves.

In this introduction let us be mindful of the fact that Australia has been in the forefront of some of the most important global environmental conflicts. These past battles have led to the recognition and declaration of numerous World Heritage Areas in Australia, the Great Barrier Reef being the first and most widely recognised.

Geography has favoured Australia in as much as it has given us challenges, such as scant rainfall over most of the nation resulting in droughts and, then as a make-even ploy, destructive cyclones. The rain they bring is compensation for inland farmers. Then there is the unique suite of biological diversity: rainforests, coral reefs, macropods and a 'bear' that is not a real bear, one that you can cuddle with the only danger being peed on. Their beauty and curiosity value are an international tourist drawcard. Note in passing that tourism and hospitality employ more Australians than any other industry. Jobs are a crucial and a potentially critical political issue in the Adani battle.

In Australia there are more UNESCO-recognised World Heritage natural areas than in any other nation. The world-wide recognition of these places, and the management regimes put in place to protect them, did not result from initiatives taken by wise Australian governments. Governments only became wise after environmental advocates fought long and successful battles to stop the despoliation of areas worthy of World Heritage status.

The word 'battles' is taken from Judith Wright's 1977 book *The Coral Battleground*. Saving the Great Barrier Reef from oil drilling and limestone mining was the first of these battles. The Great Barrier Reef became Australia's first World Heritage property. That was in 1981.

While environmental campaigners were at the forefront in the important battles, substantial public support was necessary to carry the day as battle after battle rolled on. If the most decisive action most people take in a democracy is to vote, that action can be very powerful. Votes matter to those who seek to govern. The major environmental battles were only won because a majority of citizens, as voters, wanted to protect their country's natural treasures.

In the 1960s and 1970s, environmental advocates had their requests denied, to put it mildly. Protest by standing in front of the bulldozers and expect rough treatment. There is no better example of the environmental trials and tribulations of this period than the long 19 years and 115 days of the develop-at-any-cost Queensland government, led by Bjelke-Petersen. There was one environmental fight after another: the Great Barrier Reef, Fraser Island, the Cooloola Coast, Moreton Island and the Daintree. The Great Barrier Reef, Fraser Island and the Wet Tropics (the Daintree) were to obtain World Heritage status after long, occasionally bitter and ugly, struggles between campaigners and the police sent to counter their protests.

It was not only in Queensland that confrontation occurred. The environmental campaigns in Tasmania were as long running as the Queensland ones. At times they became physical confrontational skirmishes in the forests. The battles commenced with the unsuccessful attempt to stop the flooding of Lake Pedder. It was followed by the Franklin River campaign and came to include the temperate rainforests, rivers and associated ecosystem that are known as the Tasmanian Wilderness. When it eventually came, World Heritage status was an endorsement of the environmentalists' efforts.

The campaigns to protect Australia's globally important natural areas from destructive activities, in the main mining, timber-felling and dam construction, brought to our shores eminent folk whose very presence in Australia ensured worldwide recognition of the importance, in both biodiversity terms and natural beauty, of these places. To draw from a select short-list of eminent advocates of environmentalism who visited Australia on a mission: Sir David Attenborough; David Bellamy; Al Gore. World leaders, including Bill Clinton when President of the United States, visited the Great Barrier Reef and the Wet Tropics.

With some exceptions, in particular the Hunter Valley, coal mining was not on the radar of environmental campaigners until recently. Coal mining was outback, out of sight and out of mind. When not outback, the underground mines, some burrowed under cities, with Ipswich being a good example, were as hidden as under-city sewage pipes. Coal mining remained unrecognised as an environmental matter until the connection between greenhouse gas emissions from burning coal came to be linked to climate change. The focus on coal mining and coal burning was no 'on the road to Damascus' conversion by environmental campaigners. It was gradually building up, as for quite some years there were environmentalists in sympathy with farmers in the Hunter Valley who objected to yet another coal mine. The much more recent concern with coal seam gas mining, a concern shared by farmers and urban environmentalists, gave impetus to the battle against coal mining.

By the first decade of the 21st century coal mining had taken pride of place as the major environmental issue in Australia. The Adani mine was to be the catalyst. What happens next will depend on the outcome of the battle. Our politicians will be judging the mood of electors. Financial intermediaries will be weighing up the risks of investing in coal mines (sovereign risks when governments can make dramatic about-turns; technological risks as one age closes and a new arrives). Our future is in the process of being determined.

Australia's largest coal mine, if developed, will stretch over 44,730 hectares of outback cattle country, once sheep and cattle country. Towns Australians know from school history and geography are, in outback terms, neighbours to the proposed mine. Consult any of the formal documents related to the mine and you will be informed that it is to be located 160 kilometres north-west of Clermont. Whether this means much or anything depends on your knowledge of this part of Australia. Other towns are likely to be easier to place. The largest nearby town is Emerald to the south. South-west of the proposed mine is the famous town of Barcaldine, the celebrated birthplace of the Australian Labor Party. Further west is Longreach, the town that seeks to capture the Australian outback with the Stockman's Hall of Fame. Some considerable distance north-west of the proposed mine is the town of Winton, the birthplace of Australia's national airline, QANTAS, before it was sold off. It was in this country that Banjo Paterson composed 'Waltzing Matilda'. The Adani mine is proposed in *real* Australia. Here anything is possible, but don't overstep the mark. There are natural, cultural and social characteristics that many city folk will not understand. Mr Adani will find the Australian outback alien territory.

A little physical geography is needed to locate the proposed mine. From a geological perspective the proposed mine is in the Galilee Basin. In terms of broad flora assemblages, the mine would be in the Brigalow Belt (formally known as the Brigalow Belt Bioregion), pushing into the Desert Uplands Bioregion. Notice here that common names are being converted into scientifically defined regions. Obviously, one would expect a dominance of Brigalow (Acacia harpophylla) in the Brigalow Belt, and semi-arid land in the Desert Uplands. Picture these environments of scrubby low forest and near desert, but insert into your picture veins of riverlets flowing into the Carmichael River, itself joining the Belyando River.

In association with the flowing water courses are lagoons (billabongs as Banjo Paterson called them), as likely to be fed by underground water as much as captured river flows. Later we will come to discuss the fact that the remaining Brigalow in Queensland is a threatened ecological community. Much was bulldozed or felled by large roller-balls dragged between ex-Second World War brutish machinery. New grasses were introduced. Sheep and cattle came to dominate the vast plains.

The area of the proposed mine and adjacent country is not only Brigalow. There is Gidgee (Acacia cambagei) and Mallee (Eucalyptus thozetiana), plus various other eucalypt, wattle and other species. The one eucalypt that every Australian is likely to know is the *Coolabah* tree, made famous by Banjo Paterson's 'Waltzing Matilda':

> *Once a jolly swagman camped by a billabong,*
> *Under the shade of a coolabah tree.*
> *He sang and watched and waited til his billy boiled,*
> *Who'll come a-waltzing Matilda with me.*

This land is not all stringy Brigalow and Gidgee. There are River Red Gums (E. camaldulensis) along the river banks; scattered among the sparse forest landscape are Silver-leafed Ironbark (E. Melanophlio) and Rough-leaved Bloodwood (Corymbia setosa), these being as woodland canopy species. Brown's Box (E. brownie), Dawson River Blachbutt (E. cambageana), Blackbutt (Corymbia tessellaris), and Ghost Gum (C. dallachiana) are present. The dominant species fringing the Carmichael River banks is the Weeping Paper Bark (Melaleuca Leucadendra) and in the mid-layers there are Black Wattle (Acacia salincina) and the endangered Waxy Cabbage Palm (Livistona lanuginosa). Other shrub or sparsely distributed species include Conkerrey (Carissa lanceolate), Dogwood (Acacia Coriacea), Yellowberry (Maytenus Cunninghamii), Firebark (Melaleuca nervosa), Silver Oak (Grevillea parallela), Spiny Busaria (Bursaria incana), and Townsville Wattle (Acacia leptostachya). So much for the major tree and shrub species. The grasses and herbs we will leave unrecorded. We will come to the animals that make the area home, but first a brief comment on the region's water.

The proposed mine will cut through the Carmichael River and that is a problem to which we will return. The Carmichael River is one of 29 tributaries of the Belyando River. At 1,054 kilometres in length, the Belyando River is one of the longest rivers in Queensland, a State with some quite long rivers. Given the semi-arid nature of the region, surface water ebbs and flows on the will of Mother Nature. Nevertheless, the area is blessed with the occasional ancient spring, and a series of waterholes and lagoons. Again, we should recall 'Waltzing Matilda' and the billabong where the poor sheep duffer (possibly a hungry shearer on strike) drowned. Another Paterson poem draws attention to the means by which this semi-arid country earns significant income for graziers.

In the 'Song of the Artesian Water' Paterson wrote:

Now the stock have started dying, for the Lord has sent a drought;

But we're sick of prayers and Providence – We're going to do without ...

As the drill is plugging downward at a thousand feet of level,

If the Lord won't send us water, we'll get it from the devil deeper down.

Paterson wrote of bore water from the Great Artesian Basin. With dewatering in coal mining and other uses of water in the mining process, graziers and the environment face competition for this ancient underground water. A matter for later.

The final description of the area's physical geography pertains to the habitat of the natural fauna that makes the proposed mine site home. The habitat for the following animals is within the footprint of the proposed mine: the Black-throated Finch, Ornamental Snake, Squatter Pigeon, Yakka Skink, Square-tailed Kite, Black-chinned Honeyeater, Black-necked Stork, Cotton Pygmy-goose, Little Pied Bat, Koala and Echidna. Another listing omits the Little Pied Bat but includes the Brigalow Scaly-foot. Note that migratory birds are not included in these lists, although a number do visit.

Of the above list, the Black-throated Finch is deemed to be, by both the Commonwealth and Queensland governments, an endangered species. The relevant legislation with the power to protect the bird is the Commonwealth's *Environment Protection and Biodiversity Conservation Act 1999* (*EPBC*) and the Queensland *Nature Conservation Act 1994*. The willingness to protect this bird – more so than any of the other contested matters – is likely to determine the future of the mine. Habitat suitable for the bird to relocate to has to be found and acquired. The bird has to be enticed to this new country, happy to make it its new home. This is the most important environmental offset if the mine is to operate. We know so little about the bird's response to its future if the mine goes ahead. If we could put ourselves in the bird's place we might have a good idea of the future of the proposed mine.

The pro-mining experts exude confidence that the finch will move to new territory and all will be well. This would be successful offsetting. If the Adani mine proceeds it will be the first opportunity to assess the value of offsets in delivering no loss outcomes when a major development causes significant environmental damage. Pass or fail, history will be made.

There is a substantial population of the Black-throated Finch in the proposed mine site. The mine could impact on up to 16,500 hectares of the bird's habitat. Note here that a much larger area is suggested by the Commonwealth government. Numbers, as you will come to appreciate, are the most troublesome feature of the Adani proposal. If consistency was the criterion for pass or fail, failure would be guaranteed.

To return to the Black-throated Finch, it prefers, rather needs, as habitat grassy eucalypt woodland or open woodland, especially where water and its favourite grass seeds exist. Can other suitable, nearby habitats be made available for the bird – assuming the flocks will move? What if such sites are not available? What if the bird is not to be enticed to change locations? If such matters are not resolved upfront, before habitat is destroyed, offset policies at both Commonwealth and State government level will have failed. If offsetting – that is, compensating for environmental damage – is brought into disrepute environmental management will have regressed, and then what? It will become much more difficult to have projects accepted. It is likely to be the end of offset policies. As this story unfolds, the fate of the Black-throated Finch remains unclear. Its fate could determine whether coal is mined as well as the future of environmental management in Australia.

It is not only about the finch. There are some other species in the list above that are deemed vulnerable under both the Commonwealth and Queensland legislation: the Squatter Pigeon, Yakka Skink and the Ornamental Snake. The State and Commonwealth authorities believe the habitat for these species can be managed without impacting on the animals. Whether or not that is true we won't explore here, rather suggest that the lack of solid research on the site of the proposed mine and on surrounding country means that there can be no guarantees that mitigation, adaptive management or offsets can deliver safeguards for endangered species.

Finally in this introduction, brief mention of the local land use is warranted. The proposed mine will directly impact six cattle properties. There is Moray Downs, which has been purchased by Adani. The other grazing properties are Carmichael, Mellaluka, Albinia, Doongmabulla and Lingnum. The last named is a certified organic beef producer. Some, maybe all, of these properties will be required to play an important role in providing offsets (in particular for the Black-throated Finch) if mining occurs.

I have been discussing environmental offsets without putting them into context. This I do here.

A relatively recent development in environmental management

has been the requirement to compensate for the downside of developments. Compensating has come to be called 'offsetting'.

Notwithstanding all reasonable efforts to avoid or mitigate environmental damage, there is many a project, such as a new dam, airport extension, tourism complex or large mine, that will cause 'residual damage'. This is unavoidable damage if the project goes ahead. This is the case with the proposed Adani mine and rail line.

There will be outback country dug up, grazing country lost for decades, the habitat of endangered animals and plants destroyed; there will be subsidence where underground mining extracts coal; there will be a considerable increase in greenhouse gas emissions when the coal is burned, and a non-renewable resource, the coal, will be depleted. What is the possibility of compensating for these negative effects, that is, of providing something equally valuable to that which is lost? This is what offsetting sets out to achieve.

When it was recognised that more environmental damage is inevitable if human populations continued to increase, that the world's relatively rich middle-class is being extremely slow in reducing its large ecological footprint, and that the ethical principle that the planet's poor should be helped out of poverty is to be respected, the idea of the 'compensation project' came to be accepted as the potential answer. We could continue with our lifestyles if all the adverse impacts could be offset. This is an extremely optimistic prognosis, grabbed in two hands by the optimists and doubted by the pessimists.

To date offsetting has been relatively easy. It is common to think of offsetting at a small, local scale – the mangroves removed to build a boat-ramp are offset by planting an equivalent number (it could be more) nearby. The result should be no net loss of the ecological functioning of the local mangrove ecosystem. And here is another example, an individual flying from Sydney to London can calculate her greenhouse gas emissions and give sufficient money to an offset trader who would allocate it to an organisation which would plant enough trees to extract the required quantity of carbon dioxide from the atmosphere. Put out of mind that these trees eventually die, and then what?

We are going to come to understand the Adani story in terms of the possibility of offsetting its negative impacts. This is different from the usual way of determining the likelihood that a project is worthwhile or not. The proposed mine and its associated rail line should have an upside: royalties paid to the Queensland government, to be spent on schools, health services, roadworks; income taxes paid to the Commonwealth government, to be spent on universities, CSIRO, border surveillance, and so on; and a normal profit for the mining company. I use 'should' as this is the realistic expectation of any business venture. What the actual situation turns out to be could be a vastly different scenario.

This approach allows us to explore the *prima facie* case that the venture is economically feasible and environmentally neutral (that is, the adverse effects can be compensated). This means that we will need to dig deep into the processes that, as I write, have allowed the mine to be approved by both the Queensland and Commonwealth governments. Yet, there is no certainty that Adani can meet the criteria that both governments have set it in terms of protecting the Black-throated Finch and other vulnerable, endangered species and ecosystems. The approvals to mine are conditional on offsetting successes, or so it would seem from the documented evidence. However, it will be too late if the land to be mined has been cleared and we discover the offset provisions are not working. As we will come to discover, this is a possible result.

Both governments have approved the mine and associated rail line, but a number of offset actions and programs which have to be incorporated in formal management plans have not been approved – and the possibility exists that at least some of these won't be approved when they are eventually submitted by Adani.

Even if ministers of both governments are willing to sign-off on offsets that are too vague and lacking in detail to be properly assessed (in the ministers' hurry to allow the mine to proceed), these offsets have to be made public and subject to independent professional scrutiny. Who knows what the outcome might be when interested parties get to view the offset plans. What happens if it is found to be impossible to protect the Black-throated Finch? Will the public go quietly on a flawed process?

Making offsets the framework of the analysis results in a three-pronged story. In one instance the focus will be on-site, direct environmental damage, such as loss of habitat for endangered animals and plants. Then there is damage done off-site or indirectly, such as when the coal is exported and burned overseas, as will be the case with the Adani coal. The environmental impact of burning the coal is the second part of the story. How is the resultant emission of greenhouse gases offset, if at all? The third element of the story pertains to the coal itself. Coal is for all intents and purposes a finite resource – burned and it is gone. Are future generations worse off without this source of energy? How can this be offset, assuming it should be?

2

Australia's largest coal mine

Places, people and projects have been used by historians throughout time to focus our attention on matters they deem of importance. History books help us understand our past as much as teach lessons, assuming we want to learn. There are Australian places, people and projects that will not be denied in history. One such a place is the Great Barrier Reef over which a 'battle', to use Judith Wright's word, was fought in the 1960s and 1970s, and eventually won by the environmentalists. Rather than a place, to select an environmental advocate for the history books, we cannot go past Bob Brown. He needs no introduction nor his story to be told once more.

The competition to be nominated as the standout project (that is, development) that resulted in an historic environmental dispute is stiff. There was the proposed oil-drilling on the Great Barrier Reef; the flooding of Lake Pedder; the construction of the road through the Daintree rainforests; sand-mining of Fraser Island. I am going to pass over these and some others worthy of consideration and nominate the proposed Adani coal mine as the project that will take pride of place in our history books. There are a number of good reasons to choose Adani. But first, there is the need to put the proposed mine into perspective.

The Adani coal mine, if it proceeds, will entail six open-cut and five underground mines in central Queensland, in the Galilee Basin. It would be the largest coal mine in Australia and one of the largest in the world. The coal will be transported by a purpose-built railway to a port (Abbot Point) on the boundary of the Great Barrier Reef World Heritage Area, and from there shipped to India.

It is asserted it will bring electricity to the poverty-stricken Indian slum-dwellers, of whom 240 million have no legal electricity. Slum-dwellers can do no more than steal electricity by connecting wires to the powerlines that pass overhead on their way to the enclaves of middle class and even more affluent Indians. Here, we should note a recent announcement by the World Bank: 'Solar Powers India's Clean Energy Revolution' (29 June 2017) in which it is reported 'India is emerging as a front runner in the global fight against climate change'. What is the future for coal given this prospect?

At present, one-sixth of India's electricity is provided by renewables and, according to the World Bank announcement, half will be provided by renewables by 2027. The demand for coal is expected to continue to grow up to 2027 (due to population increases and economic growth in India) but by no more than between 25 to 30%, while growth in solar-generated electricity will grow by about 250%. This is due to the fact, to once again quote the World Bank: 'it is as affordable now to generate electricity with solar power as it is with fossil fuels'. It will pay to be mindful of the World Bank's assessment when considering the prospects for the Adani mine. If the mine is to open, it will not be before the first half of the second decade of the 21st century.

The proposed Adani mine is not the only coal mine proposed for the Galilee Basin. There are nine others, including ones in the partial control of Gina Rhinehart and Clive Palmer. These household names are a guarantee that there will be considerable public focus on what happens, or is proposed to happen, in the Galilee Basin, notwithstanding the Adani proposal.

The head of the Adani enterprise, Gautam Adani, is reported to be one of the richest men in the world. He evokes a deal of negative emotion due to stories of tax avoidance, political influence and environmental mis-endeavours. A degree of investigative digging by a group of lawyers called the Environmental Justice Australia, in consort with another organisation known as Earthjustice, produced in 2017 *The Adani Files: A Short History of Corruption, Destruction and Criminal Activity*. As this report is in the public arena there is no need to deal with it here.

The Adani business model, of which we know no more than the skeleton, is centred on vertical integration – ownership of coal mines, rail lines, ports, power stations and electricity networks. The ability and the incentive to minimise tax is obvious. Transfer-pricing, in other words selling the coal at an artificial low price to show small profits in Australia, cannot be ruled out. The ability to report nothing but tiny profits in Australia means tiny royalties and tiny taxes. Both royalties and income taxes are based on profits earned in Australia.

Of course, we do not know anything of substance about the Adani business model. We can only assume that it will abide by Australian law. Presumably, it has an incentive to. To have its approval to mine revoked under Section 145 of the *EPBC Act* would end its business in Australia.

In the context of transfer pricing, Australian tax law has been strengthened recently with the imposition of the so-called 'arm's length principle'. This means that one arm of an international business that sells to another arm (inter-company business) in a low-tax country is expected to put a price on the goods or service sold that would be expected if there was no relationship between the two arms of the business. In the case of Adani, it would be expected to sell coal to its Indian-based arm at a price that, in tax jargon, reflects 'the right return for the activities [mining] carried out in Australia'.

This appears a good and sound tax principle. However, it is very new legislation and the Tax Office needs to recruit top-flight staff to undertake the necessary forensic commercial investigations. Much tax avoidance has occurred in the past, and is likely to still be occurring. There are significant incentives for transfer-pricing. The financial gains are enormous. In the Australian case much will depend on the skill of, and resources made available to, tax investigators, and in the final analysis how the courts resolve the inevitable challenges to the Tax Office. With that digression concluded we turn to another fundamental matter in the Adani story, this one central to the battle for hearts and minds.

The public protests and political campaigns against the Adani mine – on-going as this is written – are, in the main, an objection to the impact that burning coal in Indian power plants will have on the accumulation of greenhouse gases in the global atmosphere. Here is the Australian connection. Any significant increase in global greenhouse gases is considered by experts to have a dramatic adverse impact on the health of the Great Barrier Reef. It is this fear that has motivated a groundswell of objections to the opening of the mine. As a great deal has been written about this issue, we don't repeat it here but return to key aspects of this part of the story later on.

Our analysis of the Adani case brings into serious consideration the value of offsetting. Is offsetting nothing more than a 'sop' to environmentalists and the general public? Or does it, or can it, if treated seriously, maintain environmental equilibrium; in other words, leave the planet no worse off if a mine or other major development is allowed? Does a mine developer, or any other type of developer, need do no more than proclaim that offsets are part of the approval process and all will be good! 'Don't you worry about that', as one-time Queensland Premier would remark when challenged.

A reading of the Adani environmental impact statement (EIS) and related documents, such as the Queensland Coordinator-General's assessment of the EIS, leaves the reader with the impression that we are being asked to assume the job was done when the vague *announcement* of the offset policy was made. Where Adani's commitments to specific offsets have been made, they are all in the future. They are statements of what Adani will, could or might do *once it knows more about the endangered finches, waxy cabbage palms and Brigalow country.* As this story unfolds, you will discover that a general lack of knowledge, a consequence of far too little research in preparing the EIS, has frustrated all – except certain key players.

Adani's consultants, as I shall document, agree that much is unknown about the animals and plants in danger, and about the hydrology of the district. An understanding of the latter has to be a starting point for making judgements about the local impact of mining. You will discover what is not known.

With nothing more than vague promises that the offsets will

be put in place, rather than definitive offset actions approved by the Commonwealth Environment Minister and if necessary the Queensland government, and without the legal means to enforce an offsets program, is this sound public policy? Are we simply being made promises that need not be met? The fundamental question is why were water-tight offsets not in place when approval was given for the mine? As it stands, offsets can be initiated up to two years after mining commences.

Maybe I am being overly pessimistic and there will be genuine attempts to offset damage. Of course, however, attempts are one thing, success another. What if after mining has commenced, the monitoring of offsets indicates that they were poorly planned, that they were put in an inappropriate place, or they came far too late and endangered species are lost, or for any of these or other reasons fail?

It is time to outline the processes involved in the Adani case. Some have asserted that Adani has had to jump through far too many hoops, that we have witnessed 'green-tape' at its most cumbersome. This complaint does not hold up given that it was only when legal proceedings took place, after the EIS process had run its course, that crucial information was obtained from Adani. That some of this new information contradicted early claims made on behalf of Adani illustrates that every piece of green-tape, plus more, was needed to make sense of the project. And even with the conclusion of the legal proceedings, it remains unresolved how the offset programs will work.

If there has been green-tape, blame Adani for not telling a consistent, logical and complete story until the court case. It was only in the court hearings that we get an accurate count of the jobs that would be created, that we get some idea of the project's costs and benefits, flawed though they be, and some useful data on other environmental and economic aspects of the proposed mine. If there are further delays, this is because Adani has not been proactive in providing details of its offset plan.

How Adani came to acquire the rights to seek mining leases over the area in question is a story in its own right. Our story commences in November 2010 when the Queensland government (always keep in mind that this government, as representative of the people of Queensland, owns the coal) declared, rightly so, that this mine proposal required scrutiny and approval at the highest level, that means by the relevant Queensland minister of the Crown and the Co-Ordinator General, the latter considered by some as the most powerful position in the Queensland government bureaucracy. The mine plus the associated private rail line was declared a 'significant project' (otherwise a 'coordinated' project) and hence a full-blown EIS was required as the initial step if the mine was to be approved.

Not only is the approval of the government of Queensland required, the Commonwealth government has an equally powerful role. There are in the area to be mined animals and plants deemed 'endangered' under Commonwealth legislation, the *EPBC Act*. The Commonwealth term for a project that involves a high level of scrutiny is a 'controlled action'. Under a formal agreement between the Commonwealth government and the States and Territories only one EIS is required when both levels of government are empowered to decide on a particular project. And so it was in 2012 that, when Adani Mining Pty Ltd submitted its EIS, both the Commonwealth and the Queensland governments had the power to approve the mine, or not.

Throughout the ensuing years, both the Commonwealth and

Queensland governments would be a 'tag team' in assessing and finally approving the project. Here, a timeline will help with understanding the stages in the story.

The Timeline

Oct. 2010: Adani purchases EPC 1690 from Linc Energy.

22 Oct. 2010: Adani, with GHD as its consultant, provides an 'Initial Advice Statement' to the Queensland Government. [Reference: Adani Mining Pty Ltd/ GHD (2010) 'Carmichael Coal Mine and Rail Project: Initial Advice Statement', Brisbane, 2010.]

26 Nov. 2010: The Queensland Government decrees the Adani mine and rail line a 'coordinated project'.

6 Jan. 2011: The Commonwealth Government determines that the mine and rail project a 'controlled action' pursuant to the *EPBC Act 1999*.

25 May 2011: The Terms of Reference (ToR) are finalised by the Queensland government (the Coordinator-General is the lead agency). The ToR meets both Commonwealth and Queensland approval.

Nov. 2012: Adani submits its EIS.

15 Nov. 2012 to 11 Feb. 2013: The EIS is available for public perusal and comment.

26 Mar. 2013: Queensland government (Coordinator-General) requests further information from Adani to address matters raised with regard to the EIS.

25 Nov. to 20 Dec. 2013: A Supplementary EIS (SEIS) is made available for public comment.

Date unknown: Adani supplies additional information to add to the EIS (AEIS).

9 Jul.2013: Adani applies to the Queensland Department of Environment and Heritage Protection (this department regularly undergoes a name change) for a site-specific Environmental Authority for the mine.

7 May 2014: The Queensland Coordinator-General releases his evaluation of the EIS.

7 May 2014: The Queensland Coordinator-General recommends approval of the mine subject to conditions and recommendations.

24 July 2014: The Commonwealth Minister for the Environment grants approval for the mine and rail line subject to conditions. [NB. This approval is withdrawn and a new approval with conditions is granted on 14 Oct. 2014.]

28 Aug. 2014: The Queensland Environment Department (generic title) issues its Draft Environmental Authority to Adani, with conditions attached.

1 Oct. 2014: Following public notification of the mining lease application and application for an associated Environmental Authority, public objections are made to both applications. The objections are referred to the Land Court of Queensland on 1 Oct.2014.

15 Dec. 2015: The Land Court of Queensland delivers its findings and recommendations.

During 2016, Adani produces a 'Species Management Plan' and a 'Biodiversity Offsets Strategy' (BOS). The latter is commercial-in-confidence with all important information redacted. The BOS is approved by the Queensland and Commonwealth governments, although the land on which offsets are to be provided is not secured and details are not provided. A Native Title case and two Judicial Reviews are initiated by opponents to the mine. These actions result in nothing of substance changing.

During the 2017 Queensland State election campaign, the Premier announces that if her government is re-elected it will not support subsidising the Adani rail line. Adani had sought a near $1 billion loan from a special fund established by the Commonwealth government for infrastructure projects in the north of the nation. This would amount to a subsidy if granted. The Premier's decision stymies the Commonwealth government's proposal to grant the subsidy. Under an agreement between the Commonwealth and State/Territory governments the Commonwealth needs the support of the latter to make these special grants.

With the background established, we can delve into the processes that, depending on your perspective, either failed or delivered a rational result. Having stated that, be mindful that there is at the time of writing no definitive conclusion to the Adani battle. As noted earlier, and as future chapters will explore, there are hurdles that Mr Adani might be unable to clear; that is, his mine is not yet beyond the reach of the two levels of government that at this point in time have approved it on conditions he might find beyond his capabilities. Mother Nature could yet play the trump card.

The Adani case opens up for scrutiny the workings of Australia's environmental impact assessment philosophy, framework and detailed requirements. For those unfamiliar with the topic it is not the most riveting, however it is a prerequisite in unravelling the Adani story.

3

The environmental impact assessment process: warts and all

Australia was one of the first countries to accept the need for, and potential value of, environmental impact assessment. The US was the first country with an Act of Congress, in 1969. It made EISs the evaluative tool of the future, with great promise to radically change how development took place and the environment was protected.

At the Commonwealth level in Australia environmental impact assessment was introduced in 1974 when the progressive Labor government led by Gough Whitlam enacted the *Environment Protection (Impact of Proposals) Act 1974*. There were similar initiatives by some of the State governments, but legislated requirements for formal environmental impact statements were to follow the Commonwealth initiative by some years. The initial Commonwealth Act became, after a major revision and consolidation of associated laws, the *EPBC Act* in 1999.

The promise held out for EISs has been fulfilled, in part. However, with only some of the EIS's promise met, has come disappointment. One's perspective on this depends on what was expected of the EIS concept. To this matter we will come. But here we must note that the introduction of EISs was a revolution.

The EIS concept put the environment on par with the economy and society as the three reference points in the appraisal of proposed policies and projects. Then to further the revolution, in 1987 the principles of *sustainable development* were enunciated by a body of the United Nations, the World Commission on Environment and Development. As with environmental assessment, sustainable development requires the integration of ecology, economics and social/cultural factors. In addition, it introduces two over-riding principles, those of inter-generational equity and intra-generational equity. Prior to this, these principles had underpinned certain social and economic policies – in a few select countries – but were not enunciated as such. These admirable principles promise much, too much for democracies struggling to bend narrow self-interest and a myopic predisposition.

Revolutions always promise more than they can achieve, if history is a guide.

Some hoped that if a project, such as a new mine, had failed to pass a rigorous environmental assessment, the project would fail to be approved. These folks were to be disappointed. It is impossible to identify a development proposal in Australia that has been denied on the basis of an adverse conclusion in an EIS. In viewing hundreds of EISs, I have not come across one that concluded that the project be rejected.

Note that EISs are commissioned by developers, otherwise proponents of a project, and are expected to discover environmentally satisfactory ways of getting the project approved. This is why there have been many proposed projects which were redesigned so to mitigate negative impacts, and subsequently approved. This is a positive outcome of the EIS procedure. And increasingly offsetting has become integral to environmental impact assessment as developments make their way over the approval hurdles. This has been another positive initiative, when offsets opportunities have been available.

To comprehend the success of the EIS initiative, we need to go back in time to briefly reconstruct how major projects were assessed before the introduction of EISs. If they were private sector projects requiring minimum government approval (the normal case until 1970), whether the project went ahead or not depended on engineering and financial assessments undertaken by the private developer. The first thing the citizen knew about these projects was the arrival of bulldozers.

If the project was government funded, such as a new freeway, airport or dam, the appraisal would rely on engineering feasibility, costs, a budget constraint, plus some rough idea of the benefits. A new freeway would reduce traffic congestion, for a time, and this was a benefit. A new dam would allow agriculture to expand, again a benefit. In the 1950s in the US, rudimentary cost-benefit analysis started to be used as an assessment tool. However, environmental costs (and benefits if any) tended to be neglected. The tools that economists needed to measure 'externalities', such as environmental damage, were still on the drawing board.

A number of environmental disasters involving the grounding of oil tankers, and the consequential oil spills which suffocated sea birds and wreaked havoc with local fisheries, provided disturbing television images and became the catalyst to include the environment (that which no one, rather everyone, owned) as an integral component of project assessments. There was no going back, the environment was to be on par with the economy, and numerous partly successful attempts were made to marry the two disciplines of ecology and economics. What helped the process, although ultimately it failed to achieve its goal, was the definition of 'the environment' to include humans, their economy and society. The incorporation of economic and social benefits and costs into EISs tends to be poorly done.

The EIS process was by design open to public input. However, it cannot be claimed that it was to provide public participation in a meaningful sense. This notion is a contested one, ranging from the utopian idea of a modern Greek 'agora' and its associated participatory democracy (unless if you were a female or a slave), through to the occasional plebiscite (a formal public opinion poll). In the formulation of the EIS concept, the public was granted rights to comment – and in certain cases to initiate legal challenges and be involved in court hearings – but the final decision as to the approval or disapproval of a project rested with either a government minister or high-ranking public bureaucrats. Even courts, if they are like the one we come to discuss later, the Queensland Land Court, are constrained in what power they have, confined to giving advice to government ministers, rather than to making the ultimate decision. This is the case for mining matters, where the court plays an administrative role rather than a judicial one.

Regardless of the nature of public involvement, the EIS process promised transparency and has gone some way in providing it. A crucial matter is the nature of the subject matter that is dealt with in an EIS. If it is not related to what is of concern to the public, the value of transparency is questionable. Encyclopaedic lists of commonly known plants and animals in the area of a project, such as a mine, give the impression of considerable research, but if these are not impacted this is a waste of space in an EIS.

The final product of a comprehensive assessment of a project, always undertaken by a consultant, tends to be an enormous report, full of detail, but more likely than not that some, or even much, of the detail is superfluous, while the essential detail required if the public is to be informed, so to allow for a rational evaluation, is most likely to be omitted. We will illustrate this with reference to the Adani case. The public wants to know if the project 'stacks up' in environmental and economic terms. It looks for decisive, evidence-based conclusions.

Making environmental matters equivalent in status to financial and engineering ones, bringing the public into a quasi-decision-making position and introducing a level of transparency, were and remain positive outcomes of formal environment impact assessment. Still, in practice the EIS tool is falling short of its promise. This is evident in the Adani case. In part this is a result of the erroneous information provided by Adani to both its environmental consultant and the Queensland government. It is a fact that on some issues, particularly ones to do with the expected number of jobs and the life of the project, a consultant is in the hands of the proponent's experts who commission the EIS. Government employees who write the terms of reference for an EIS are also reliant on the information provided to them by the developer, in our case Adani.

The matter of directing an environmental consultant to the crucial tasks to be investigated and reported on in an EIS should not be left in the hands of a developer, for obvious reasons. This is common practice.

In part the flaws in the Adani EIS result from the modelling undertaken by Adani. Then, there was the disproportionate amount of space given over to so-called 'economic impact' with no analysis of whether the costs of the project are justified by its benefits. Only by doing the latter type of analysis can the need for the mine be determined.

A focus on 'economic impact' has come to be associated with calculating local and regional jobs, as well as direct (mine-related) and indirect (flow-on) output and income. Of course, local jobs and business opportunities are important. Because the proposed Adani mine and rail-line construction is organised on a fly-in, fly-out basis, the vast majority of workers are likely to reside in coastal towns. The analysis and description of the local economic impact of the project should have been a relatively minor and brief matter. What has taken the interest of various interested parties, including the general public, is the amount of money as royalties and taxes that would flow to the Australian people if the mine went ahead. And whether or not the benefits could in some way *compensate* for the inevitable negative impacts, if they could not be offset.

The 'economic impact' approach does not inform anyone of the economic viability of the mine or the social costs and benefits; this approach allows the mine's owner to keep to himself matters such as the profitability of the mine. Still, an immediate reaction could be: 'well, that is Mr Adani's business and not to be shared on commercial-in-confidence grounds'. There is no argument with this proposition, if the project was, say, a tourist resort where the developer owned the land and there were no non-priced costs to others (for example, no mangroves were to be felled and hence no loss of fish catches). This is far from the case of the Adani coal mine.

A coal mine, and other types of mining, are using up the

resources owned by the public. Governments on our behalf *invite* prospective miners to dig up the coal or whatever else, on the grounds that we, the owners, get a fair economic return. In the case of coal in the State of Queensland that return is based on the profits made by the miner. Only by knowing what the profits are expected to be, given the vagaries of markets, can a government estimate whether it is worth allowing mining, and make realistic budget forecasts. Keep in mind that government treasurers factor in expected royalties when making budget estimates.

That mining in the State of Queensland has to be economically viable is stated in law. The *Mineral Resources Act 1989* puts this up front in its 'Objectives' [Section (2e)]. The relative objective is to 'ensure an appropriate financial return to the State from mining'. On this basis, one would expect royalties to be in concert with the profits that could be expected to be earned if the coal was mined by the government. The government-as-miner would take all the risks. Like a private enterprise mine, the government would borrow funds (at a cheaper rate than a private burrower) and pay interest and return the capital. The Australian situation of taking a share of the profits as royalties is a way of sharing the risk and sharing the profits. It is not for us here to discuss and debate the setting of coal royalties in Queensland. One can only hope that the folk who undertake this task are out to do the strongest business deal possible for the public.

4

What's the mine about?
Are the poor in India to benefit?

Australian universities have been teaching environmental assessment courses from the late-1970s, that is, for 40 or so years. One might expect that all the initial rough edges have been smoothed out. Not so, a matter we will come to. In the main, the early university EIS subjects were targeted to what manner of subject-matter (for example, water quality, noise pollution, job creation) were to be assessed, as well as the formal requirements by which to report the results. The assessment methods, such as ecological fieldwork and desk-based deciphering of census data, were taught in discipline-specific subjects in the same degree. And this was generally the case for the scientific tools to be used in specific situations. With a focus on process and content (the subject matter), the guide to the curriculum was the existing legislation, such as the *Environment Protection (Impact of Proposals) Act 1974*.

In recent years, governments have published specific guides on how to undertake an EIS, and what to include. Then for specific projects, such as the Adani one, requiring joint Commonwealth–State assessment, specific terms of reference are prepared. We will refer to relevant government guidelines in establishing what should have been the case in assessing the Adani mine and rail project. To a certain degree, the fact that some years after the formal EIS procedure finished we are still debating the mine suggests that the guidelines might not have been tight enough. That it took the court case to obtain crucial information from Adani indicates that the EIS guidelines should have been stricter.

Given that the Adani mine and rail project is to be in Queensland, the first guide in preparing an EIS would be the Queensland government's 'Generic draft terms of reference for an environmental impact statement'. However, the senior Adani staff overseeing the EIS preparation and the consultant who undertook it would have been instructed by the 'guide' referred to below, as well as the specific terms of reference for the Adani project. If these guides had been followed, and the correct information provided by Adani, there should not have been shortcomings in the Adani EIS. To these we will come.

The Queensland government's generic terms of reference for EISs makes it clear that one of the first things to be discussed in an EIS is the project's 'objectives' – otherwise its goals, aims, what it is to achieve. The requirement immediately following asks that the 'rationale for the project' be given. The idea underpinning this is that the public deserves to be told what is going to be achieved by the project. This has the potential to circumvent unnecessary debate.

Consider this: Is the Adani mine going to change the material living conditions of hundreds of millions of the poorest of the poor Indians, as we see in public statements? Or is simply to meet increasing demand for thermal coal in India, demand that is increasing because the Indian middle-class is increasing in numbers? Your attitude with regard to the mine is likely to be quite different depending on the answer. The *objective* of a project can be a turning point in terms of public support.

The objectives of some projects are obvious: a new hospital will treat the ill and a new school will teach pupils, and in both cases without any negative impacts, while a new mine will produce ores/minerals but there are likely to be negative impacts to be weighed against the positive ones.

Apologies for labouring the requirement to require an upfront discussion of what the project aims to achieve. It is a fundamental requirement if an EIS is to play its designated societal role. A clear, unambiguous, informative statement of objectives is often neglected or even treated with distain in EISs. I can suggest one reason for this. Some proponents of projects are inclined to the predisposition, Why should I have to justify my project? Any proposal requiring an EIS is likely to need to explain to the public what it aims to provide. Undoubtedly, a project such as the Adani mine, which aims to profit from selling *our* coal, is obliged to be upfront on all matters of public interest, and that includes what it aims to do with the coal.

What is the goal of the Adani mine? In an examination of the vast number of formal reports pertaining to the mine, the answer to this question is not obvious – except at a superficial level. I accept on face value Mr Adani's statement of 5 February 2018 that his Carmichael coal mine will help bring power to 18,000 villages (*Courier Mail*, 5 February 2018). But I take it as axiomatic that as a businessman Mr Adani wants to make money, to become richer, from the development of this mine.

Reverting back to the matter of what the Adani EIS should have done, another EIS guide I would expect to have been consulted is the Queensland government's 2015 publication 'Preparing an environmental impact statement: Guideline for proponents'. In its words it requires 'a clear outline of the objective'; and then it makes the point that it is necessary to answer the following question: What are 'the consequences of not proceeding with the action (otherwise, project)'? What is foregone? Indian villagers without electricity. No royalties for the Queensland government. These are the types of arguments one would have expected, backed up with real numbers. In the same document, this requirement is otherwise referred to as 'the alternative of taking no action' (that is, not proceeding with the project). There can be no clearer statements to treat the justification of the mine seriously.

The failure to identify the objectives of the project can be put on the shoulders of Adani. Notwithstanding this, the government agency responsible for the preparation and assessment of the EIS has a duty to require adherence to the law and policies it administers. Proponents need to be brought to bear when they are off-handed in not addressing the need or no action alternative. To foreshadow a discussion in a future chapter, Adani can claim to have addressed this question by arguing that if the Queensland mine is disallowed the coal will be sourced elsewhere. While this probably the case, Adani still has the task of convincing the Queensland owners of the coal that allowing Adani to mine it is a worthwhile deal for them. This should have been attempted in the EIS. Otherwise what is the point of the substantial expenditure in preparing an EIS!

Again foreshadowing this future discussion, Adani has in-advertently done a poor job in convincing Queenslanders, and for that matter their fellow Australians, that its mine is a good deal. When a business goes searching for subsidies eyebrows are raised. Adani asked for a no-interest loan of near $1 billion, a Townsville rate-payer funded airport at a cost of $18.5 million, and a royalty holiday for two years. That two of these requests have, after initial acceptance, been denied Adani does not alter the fact that a supposedly profitable venture, which promises royalties and taxes, is counting on subsidies from those to whom it was to pay.

Bob Katter, the flamboyant wearer of big hats, who happens to be a federal member of Parliament representing a large slice of north Queensland, found cause to condemn the request for a tax-payer subsidy in these terms: 'If the foreign corporation needs $18.5 million, then I think we can safely assume the project [the mine] is in real trouble' (*Courier Mail*, 22 January 2018).

To make clear that explaining the rationale for the project and identifying its beneficiaries is a universal EIS requirement, here is an example from the NSW 2017 guide 'Preparing an Environmental Impact Statement':

> 'Proponents must state the key objectives of the project and … how the project meets these objectives. This … should simply state why the project is being proposed and what the benefits are.' Note 'what the benefits are'.

Read on in this document and it is made clear that the benefits have to be compared to the costs.

Finally, we come to the particular terms of reference in the EIS for the Adani mine and rail project. These are to be found in the Queensland government's (2011) 'Carmichael Coal Mine and Rail Project: Final terms of reference for the environmental impact statement'. Under the heading 'Project Rationale' we read that the proponent has to 'Describe the specific objective and justification for the project, including its strategic, economic, environmental and social implications …' These are important, quite basic and, if treated seriously, relatively easy to deal with requirements of the EIS. What does one find in the Adani EIS?

The EIS, which would appear to be a joint effort by Adani and its consultant, is extremely brief in discussing the objectives of the project. Here it is:

> The primary objective of the Project is to produce 60 Mtpa of thermal coal product for export to meet demand for coal in India … Adani Enterprises Limited sees supply from Queensland coal resources as key to meeting its target of generating 20,000 MW of power from its power plants by 2020. If the project does not proceed it would likely lead to Adani's demand for coal being met outside of Australia and the benefits of significant economic investment would not be released.

And: 'The Project also presents a range of opportunities and positive impacts to regional and State economies.'

This statement by Adani relates to its business interests. We would expect nothing else if the development of the mine and rail line was solely Adani's business. Let us imagine Adani owned the land under which the coal existed, also owned the coal, owned the water which would be used in the process of mining, the land the rail-line would traverse, and that there were no negative impacts on anyone else from mining and transporting the coal. In this hypothetical situation we might say 'go ahead Mr Adani and mine'. None of this hypothetical situation is the case.

The citizens of Queensland own the coal, the water in the ground below the coal, the surface water which flows over the mine site, and the grazing land on which the mine will sit (held in leasehold by graziers). The property rights held by the people of Queensland mean that Adani has to convince the government (as the people's representative) that Adani should be granted a right to extract and export coal.

The initial question is: Does the statement of objectives quoted above satisfy the people of Queensland? Clearly, the author cannot know the answer to this question, but suggests that Queenslanders would expect some level of financial benefits from the mine, as a 'starter', as they say in negotiating deals. As noted above, Mr Adani goes as far as suggesting a loss of benefits to Queenslanders and other Australians if the mine is disallowed. He states that if the mine is disallowed, he would seek coal elsewhere. This, presumably, implies a loss for Queenslanders and other Australians. Yet we are not provided through the EIS process with sufficient information to make that assessment. Are we simply witnessing a bluff? One that our decision-makers have fallen for.

A proposal like Adani's, where the opposition to it is strong, can be made to look good if the understandable self-interest of the proponent is ignored and the mined coal is going to be used to change the lives of millions for the better. This is what Mr Adani claimed in the newspaper story referred to above. He is not the only advocate for the mine to argue that changing the lives of the poor of India is the aim of the project. There are Australians who paint Mr Adani's coal mine enterprise as the next best thing to philanthropy.

A Steve Knott, in a media release on behalf of the Australian Resources and Energy Group, wrote the following on 12 May 2017:

> In India, there are hundreds of millions of people living in what most of the developed world would consider

impoverished conditions ... there are millions of people in India still cooking with solid fuels like wood, animal dung and crop waste ... the Adani project ... will ... provide basic electricity needs for hundreds of millions of Indians ...

And here is Judith Sloan writing about the Adani mine in the *Australian*: 'Think of the benefits ... for India, a country were more than 300 million live without electricity'.

This pulling at the heartstrings has to be seen for what it is – a nonsense! We need to understand that the poor – in fact, very poor – in India cannot afford to purchase electricity that is produced by coal if it is sold at market-based prices. This is recognised by the Indian central government and for this reason farmers and village centres get subsidised electricity, but individuals who cannot afford to pay for electricity go without.

We should not be blind to the pitiful lives of India's poor. Organisations like the World Bank, the Asian Development Bank and the United Nations Development Program provide data on the percentage of Indians who fall below the standard benchmarks of extreme poverty, US$1.25 per person/day based on purchasing power parity or the more lenient US$1.90 per person/day based on the same adjustment. Somewhere between one fifth and one quarter of Indians fall into these categories. This is, not unexpectedly, the same percentage without mains electricity.

According to a World Bank group report (27 May 2016), India's poor spend the bulk of their income on food (56%) and little on fuel and light. Kerosene is purchased if it can be afforded otherwise wood and animal dung are used for cooking, and the setting of the sun means total darkness. The poor can but dream of air-conditioning in the extreme heat of summer. The only means of electric power for these people is the theft of electricity, stolen by hooking a wire to an overhead power line. If undertaken by the desperately poor, this can be understood and even justified.

If the Adani mine is to play a dominate role in relieving electricity poverty in India, the case needs to be explained in sufficient detail, not asserted as a fact by people like Judith Sloan, who as an economist should be far more careful in coming to judgement. If she is serious about the future of the Indian poor there is much to be learned by spending time in the country, studying the great inequality in the distribution of power, of land, of income, and the perverse role of the caste system. Before going into print, she might have asked herself this question: If Adani is to spend a total of about $120 billion over 56 years (40 million tonnes mined on average per year, over 56 years, at a cost of $50 tonne including interest and profits) which equates to just over $2 billion a year, each year, disregarding discounting, what alternative project could that money be used for if it was to bring electricity to the poor? As an alert reader you will have noticed that I used 40 million tonnes per annum, not the 60 million tonnes reported before. Where did the smaller number come from? None other than Dr Fahrer, Adani's expert economist, giving evidence to the Land Court. Nothing changes but Adani's numbers.

This is a question that all parties involved in this dispute should have asked. If the objective is to bring electricity to the poor of India, what are the options (alternatives in the EIS sense)? This is what students in EIA 101 are taught to ask. Start with a very broad objective and often, not always, a range of alternatives will exist. Choose the least costly one if it provides the same benefits as the others.

We must recognise that Mr Adani has not set out to solve

energy poverty in India. His objective is to make money. If we are to support his mine, let us be honest about his objective – and ours.

This means that we must recognise that the Queensland government does not want to forgo potentially significant royalties from selling coal. Those potential royalties are a benefit to us, the owners of the coal. The Queensland government faces in a very difficult situation. And so do we as beneficiaries of royalties and taxes if the mine is profitable, a matter we will come to. How this money, if it were to eventuate, is used is as important.

Put yourself in the position of the Queensland government. You and I realise that the coal age is likely to end while there is still coal in the ground. The technological advances in renewable energy and the threat of severe climate change are sound reasons to believe in the coming end of the coal age. Herewith, the ethical and financial dilemma. If there is global demand for coal and we have it, do we refuse to sell coal and forego the money to be earned, while others are more than willing to sell it. Or do we take an ethical path and say no to mining and the money! These are the options faced by the Queensland government.

We know that the Queensland government is aware of the threat to the Great Barrier Reef from global warming, and that it carefully considers the value of making a statement to the world by what it does. The advice that has been provided to the Queensland government after the extensive environmental assessment processes, involving a formal EIS and court hearing, is to allow the mine. As a politician, a representative of the people who own the coal, what do I do? I could neglect the formal advice that I have asked for and been given. I could review that advice and deem it to be faulty, and on that basis reject the mine, or seek further scientific investigation before making a decision.

In a future chapter I shall analyse the conclusions reached by Carmel MacDonald, President of the Land Court at the time of the Adani hearings. Regardless of the findings made by the President, the evidence presented to the Court in support of the mine is such that its benefits have not been proven beyond a reasonable doubt. In line with the propositions expressed at the beginning of this book, there remains scope for you dear reader to come to your own conclusion and influence the final decision.

Before it becomes necessary for the public to have an explicit say, there are still hoops that the Adani project faces in terms of meeting offset conditions, particularly with regard to the survival of the Black-throated Finch and 'making good' on withdrawal of ground water. Can we be confident that the mine will proceed? And, there is still unresolved as I write the small matter of Mr Adani obtaining finance. He is a modern entrepreneur. He needs willing financiers.

I discovered an insightful comment on the Adani business model which makes for an appropriate closing comment for this chapter. Malcolm Turnbull, the Prime Minister, has summed up the objective of the Adani project better than anyone else: 'He [Adani] is going to be producing coal, most of which he will be buying himself to fuel his own power stations in India' (*Weekend Australian*, 12 April 2017).

Turnbull did not make the obvious statement that this type of vertical integrated commercial arrangement is the prerequisite for transfer pricing – using 'in-company' prices throughout the value-added chain to minimise tax. One can imagine the coal leaving Australia being sold at a price below its true cost of production, the purchaser being a power station in India. As a result, above-normal profits will accrue in India where Adani has the ability to pay a lower tax rate than in Australia. I don't suggest this is what Adani aims to do – a point I have made previously – but the vertical integration that Turnbull refers to makes easily for that possibility.

In the next chapter we focus on how the EIS deals with economic matters. Information that has escaped others, including critics of the Adani, is brought to bear.

5

How do we know the mine is worth it?

The environmental impact assessment process was designed to inform the public of the positive and negative aspects of a development, and thus allow for informed public comment. Via this process, projects have been modified to achieve better environmental outcomes, and in theory the public should be able to stop a project if it has the necessary evidence to achieve that outcome. That means that an EIS should deal with pertinent matters in a way that lay people can understand them. Those charged with preparing the terms of reference for an EIS should have a reasonable understanding of the matters that interest the public.

The last thing we want is the developer setting the terms of reference for an EIS that its chosen consultant will undertake. This practice was noted in the previous chapter. Here, we can note that on 13 January 2018, the *Weekend Australian* carried an advertisement on behalf of the Queensland and Commonwealth governments informing the public that the Draft Terms of Reference for an EIS on the prosed Walton Coal Project was available for comment. The proposed mine, for metallurgical coal, would be in central Queensland. The concern is that the coal mining company has drafted the terms of reference. Of course, the terms could be excellent. That is not an issue. The problem is that our government officers, expert in dealing with EIS requirements, have not been given the job that only impartial folk can do.

The public's strong interest in a particular subject might not be deemed crucial by those who write the terms of reference. This is no reason to leave the matter or matters of public concern out. Ignore what is stirring the public, and the EIS is irrelevant in the political battle that will ensue. Furthermore, there will be in the long-term diminished public respect for EISs. This would be a serious regression in environmental management.

If, as is the case with the Adani mine, the most widely held concern is the adverse impact on the health of the Great Barrier Reef, it should have been dealt with up front. Even if the burning of coal overseas was deemed beyond the scope of the EIS, a matter discussed below, this should have been stated up front. I have noted a reluctance to deal with the environmental impact overseas of Australian products and commodities. If this remains the case, for better or worse, there is a requirement for another process to deal with the so-called 'extra-territorial' impacts. The impact of carbon emissions when Australian coal is burned in India could have been handled outside of the EIS process. This would have required Australian governments, both Commonwealth and State/Territory, to have opened up a public debate on extra-territorial impacts.

The most basic questions for this debate are: Who is responsible for adding to global warming, the producer (in our case, Australia) or the consumer (middle-class Indian electricity users)? Is it realistic to impose caveats on foreign purchasers of our coal, such as coal can only be burned if carbon capture and sequestration is undertaken? This idea, not feasible at present, is borrowed from the international protocols surrounding the export of uranium.

What is the strength of the ethical message sent out to the rest of the world if we decide that we will not mine any more coal? Who will take notice and possibly fall in behind us? Ethical stances should not be dismissed out of hand. Investors take note when the Norwegian sovereign-wealth fund sells its holding in firms that are deemed to be unethical. Australia does not have the same claim to international fame that Norway does. To these matters we will return as the debate is much more nuanced. My point here is that we should not expect an EIS to deal with and resolve extra-territorial matters when their solution is both an ethical and political task, not to be resolved by the scientific analysis we expect in an EIS.

To the credit of the President of Queensland Land Court, who heard the objections to the Adani mine, the global warming resulting from the burning of the coal in India was addressed, though not to the satisfaction of the objectors.

The matter of extra-territorial impacts remains alive as far as objectors to the mine are concerned – after a near decade of campaigning. Not only is it the fundamental debate with regard to the Adani mine, it will be the basis of objection to the other nine proposed mines in the Galilee Basin. Better late than never, the matter needs to be subject to informed public debate in anticipation of the objections to these other coal mines. Extra-territoriality is not a new issue – having been raised with regard trade and trade sanctions and environmental pollution over many decades – but the philosophical and practical aspects need revisiting, even if there is no change to the principle and practice.

In Australia, the extra-territorial debate first occurred when the mining of export Australian uranium was examined in the 1970s by a formal commission of inquiry under the *Environment Protection (Impact of Proposals) Act 1974*. The result was that uranium mined in Australia was allowed to be exported to countries that undertook not to use it for military purposes.

Many countries have faced the same dilemma – selling abroad something that when put to final use will cause environmental or other damage. An early attempt to deal with this issue was undertaken by the OECD in the 1970s when it made the 'polluter-pays' the philosophical principle. Under this principle, the polluter is not the producer but the user. Hence, the principle becomes the 'user-pays' principle.

No sooner had this is principle been recognised than a converse philosophy came to be applied to the international trade in illegal drugs. Drug traders are deemed the criminals. On the other hand, the drug users are treated leniently. There must be scope to re-examine the 'user-pays' principle as it is applied in all manner of circumstances, including the export of fossil fuels.

The argument for Australia refusing to export more coal may be put in terms of both ethics and self-interest. In the latter regard, it is asserted that the economic value of the Great Barrier Reef to the Australian economy is of much greater magnitude than coal royalties and taxes. A refusal to sell thermal coal (coal to fire power stations) to illustrate that the Australian people care more for the Great Barrier Reef could resonate at a global scale. In the Adani case this very point was argued by opponents of the mine throughout the appraisal process, all the way into the formal court proceedings, which took place five years from the commencement of the assessment process.

Mindful of this discussion and the suggestions made, we must deal with the situation as it exists at this point in time. So to the practice.

As noted above, EIS laws and policies require the proponent to answer – usually at the outset – what the project aims to achieve, and answer the question, If it is permitted to go ahead will there be an overall benefit to society? However, these matters tend to be down-played. On the other hand, there is a tendency to spend much time and resources in obtaining and reporting rather basic information (ecological, social and economic) on the local area – some of which is pertinent, but much of it unnecessary.

In the case of the Adani mine, the EIS did not address the most basic matters that exercised the minds of its opponents, such as the addition to greenhouse gases with the burning of the coal overseas, or the level of royalties and income taxes accruing to Australians. If an EIS does not deal with matters the public seeks information on, or if fails to convince the public, the project is likely to become a festering political sore. This can be the case even though public servants and government ministers on reviewing the EIS are convinced the project is worthwhile. Who is right, the public or the decision-makers?

If senior public servants and government ministers come to a different conclusion from that of the interested public, this is likely to be for one or other of the following reasons: the decision-makers have put much more effort in studying the project than anyone else, and have the knowledge to make a better-informed decision; or, the government (ministers and senior public servants) have convinced themselves on other grounds that the project is warranted. The latter case could be because lobbyists have been successful, or because the decision-makers have an ideological predisposition to favour 'development' regardless of its overall merits. And, of course, one cannot rule out local versus state-wide and national politics. It is to be expected that media outlets in the proximity of the mine will make its approval a local political issue.

Let us explore what an EIS is supposed to do in justifying or not a project.

Here is one of many similar statements of what a properly conducted EIS is to do:

> The EIS should end with an evaluation of the project as a whole, drawing conclusions on the overall merits of the project. A detailed analysis of the EIS should be 'weaved' into a coherent closing discussion. The proponent should describe how the project, compared with other alternatives, balances impacts, strategic need, benefits and is in the public interest … the conclusion should address the following … weighing up of the main environmental impacts (costs and benefits) associated with the project … whether, on balance, the impacts and benefit of the proposal favour the public interest. (NSW Planning & Environment, 2017, p. 16)

The role and influence of the key parties is likely to frame an EIS in terms of what issues it gives pride-of-place to, what matters it skates over, and the type of analyses applied. Who supplies the basic data is crucially important. It is important to note that it is the proponent (for example, the mine developer), not the consultant contracted by the developer to prepare the EIS, who has to provide certain key data (overwhelmingly the case for economic data).

Data is very important because it is the building block of various types of analyses. An EIS is expected to come to robust, evidence-based conclusions. Both the evidence presented by the proponent to his/her consultant and the evidence the consultant gathers in the field are likely to be inputs into modelling exercises, to go from the specific to the overall picture.

However, the type of modelling undertaken can exert considerable influence on the results of an analysis. This is very obvious in the economic modelling for the Adani mine. Adani's model set out to answer one set of questions. The objectors to the mine relied on a completely different model to answer different questions. That this happens is a flaw in the evaluation process. It was only discovered in the court hearing. This is when Adani's man changed his mind on the number of jobs to be created, from 10,000 to 1,464! Imagine the consequences if this modelling error had not been discovered. Investors would have been building motels in Clermont, new grocery stores, houses in Rockhampton and Yeppoon. All wasted money.

Allow me to digress. Mining booms affect social psychology. The vast majority who come under the influence of a boom spend as if the world is coming to an end, regardless of the fact that they live thousands of kilometres from the mines. Our governments do the same thing, a matter coming up. The vast majority of Australians have never seen a mine and are unlikely too. The media is the source of their knowledge.

I travelled through the coal-seam gas country of Queensland and northern NSW a number of times during the 'boom'. This was when the pipeline to Gladstone was being laid. It was near impossible to acquire short-term accommodation in the very average highway motels or the few remaining country pubs that offered a bed and breakfast. Fly-speck towns that survived on graziers' monthly grocery orders and came to life during the local shearing season, now all but gone as cattle replaced sheep, overflowed with workers laying the gas pipelines. I drove past town after town in search of a vacant motel room or caravan in a riverside caravan park. Digression complete, but keep in mind that large numbers are not needed to mine coal. Coal-mine development is very different from installing a number of coal-seam gas wells on one property after the other and then laying a very long pipeline to the east coast town of Gladstone.

There are numerous problems with any last-minute disagreement and debate over fundamental issues, particularly if they are make-or-break ones, which could be the case for the Adani mine. That noted, the major problem in the Adani case was that a lawyer, the President of the Land Court, was put in the unenviable position of having to untangle economic data, models and conclusions based on completely different approaches. One approach happened to be the correct one. Did she know which one was the correct one? Did she make the right decision?

Had these contrasting economic modelling exercises been in the EIS, published well before the Adani case got to court, one would have expected that economists in the relevant government departments to have identified the problem and requested both Adani and its opponents to come to a professional agreement on the appropriate modelling. Much angst would have been avoided and maybe the key decision-makers would have come to different decisions on the mine.

Here another brief digression is warranted. There is an adage from the early days of computing which remains relevant to the present: GIGO, otherwise *garbage-in, garbage-out*. It is the job of the experts in the government authority who write the terms of reference for a EIS to ensure that appropriate data is fed into the models. The inexplicable error in the estimate of jobs created is likely to have resulted from inaccurate data fed into the model, as well as model assumptions about the operation of local projects in a state-wide and national economy.

This is getting ahead of the story, but the evidence is on the public record, as will be presented, that Adani was able to get away with serious distortions of economic reality in the EIS (and its supplements) until the court case. The economic distortions were so serious that had they been identified in the early days, the project might have been curtailed at that stage. The proponent would have had little credibility as a business. A reputable business organisation does not make outlandish claims – certainly does not publish numbers that play into the hands of its opponents. Only through the intervention by economists commissioned by opponents to the mine were the serious errors uncovered, and this was after the EIS had run its course and both sides had to argue their cases in court.

That people of influence continued to act as if the distortion had not occurred is a puzzle. Yet there is worse. Some eminent people, politicians in particular, continue to this day to repeat the faulty employment data knowing that it has been refuted by Adani itself, not by its opponents. The standout example is the assertion of 10,000 jobs resulting from the project. When the error was uncovered in the Land Court hearing, it was corrected by an Adani advocate. This was widely reported in the daily news. There can be no excuse of not knowing this fact.

Time to move on.

One of the most basic questions in environmental, and all public policy matters, is how to determine what is 'the public interest'. If this is a matter of weighing costs and benefits, there is the other basic question of how to measure costs and benefits. Economists believe they have the answer and the tools for the latter task. Some will argue that the public interest is determine by cost-benefit analysis; however, there are practical and philosophical objections to the use of the economists' method.

The idea of the public interest has long played a role in the armoury of environmental advocates and environmental lawyers. In the early to mid-1970s, fierce defenders of coastal ecosystems battled miners of the black beach sands. John Sinclair and his organisation FIDO appealed against every mining lease application on Fraser Island, arguing the public interest equated to saving the island untouched for its natural beauty and eco-tourism values. Others campaigned just as rigorously to protect Cooloola, Agnes Waters and Moreton Island from the miners. In those days there was no special court to which one could appeal against a grant of a mining lease. Magistrates empowered as Mining Wardens heard the cases. The rapidly evolving understanding of biodiversity values and the emerging nature-based tourism experience were matters not familiar to a local magistrate who would spend most of his time dealing with minor traffic offences or misbehaviour by drunks. It proved impossible to convince a mining warden that beaches and dunes were valuable if left to nature.

Appeals against mining were lost in these quasi-courts but won on the power of public opinion – this in an era when Queensland was governed by a 'develop-at-any-cost' Premier, Joh Bjelke-Petersen. That public opinion prevailed (with on occasion the help of the Commonwealth government, which had the power to stop the export of the mineral sands) is a wonder. Fraser Island, Moreton Island and most of the wave-washed beaches as far north as the Town of 1770 were saved, with Fraser Island to become a World Heritage Area.

One of the consequences of these sand-mining disputes was that the matter of defining the public interest went to the High Court in 1975. It is a case that is commonly quoted – and is referred to by the Land Court President in the Adani case. Here is a non-lawyer's interpretation of the judgment in *Sinclair v the Ming Warden at Maryborough*: the concept of public interest is very wide, but the size of the community having a concern with the issue (say, mining beaches) is fundamental to the applicability of a public interest test. The greater the number of people who are potentially affected, the more likely there is a question of public interest. This would suggest to me that the public interest would have to be taken into account in the Adani case. A very large community, the Australian taxpayers and the Queensland public, have a direct financial interest and potentially diverse environmental interests in the outcome.

Australian lawyers rely on precedents, decisions by judges, as to the meaning of the public interest. This, as we will see in terms of the Adani case, is the beginning and end of the matter for the lawyers. On the other hand, political theorists and economists have their own ways of defining the public interest. You would be justified in being concerned that there can be no unambiguous decision on contested environmental issues if there is no agreed way to compare the good to the bad and settle on *the* public interest.

I have to return to the matter of 'need' as a fundamental

requirement of the EIS process. To some extent this has already been done above; however, the concept is so important that additional treatment is warranted here.

There are various ways of wording the requirement to determine the need for a project. The Queensland government in its 'Preparing an environmental impact statement: Guidelines for proponents' (2015) requires consideration of 'the consequences of not proceeding with the action [project]'. Elsewhere in this guide it puts this requirement in roughly similar terms by requiring an analysis of 'the alternative of taking no action'; in other words, not opening the mine.

As there were specific terms of reference for the Adani mine and rail project, an independent observer is likely to turn to them for guidance. In document titled 'Carmichael Mine and Rail Project: Final terms of reference for the environmental impact assessment' (2011, p. 11) the following is under the sub-title 'Objectives of the EIS': 'provide public information on the need for the project, alternatives to it and options for its implementation'.

Elsewhere in this guide we find helpful elaboration. For example, alternatives to the mine have to be 'feasible and prudent'; there is to be included in the EIS 'a framework for decision-makers to assess the environmental aspects'. Note that the Adani EIS contains nothing which could be deemed a decision-making framework. A framework would have certainly assisted the decision-makers and the interested public.

However, it could be argued that the folk who prepared the terms of reference should have set the framework, not leave it to Adani or its consultant. Those who established the terms of reference are, presumably, experts in establishing an evaluation framework that suits their purposes; they deal with a vast array of projects year in, year out and should have this matter down pat. On the other hand, project proponents and their consultants will do no more than what is required of them, and they cannot be expected to give attention to matter that has the potential to shine a negative light on their project. If there is to be a genuinely independent and robust framework, the ball must be in the court of government officials to construct that framework.

In the terms that politicians and the media focus on, the mine is 'needed' (otherwise justified) if it generates jobs, the more the merrier. Job creation is an economic matter. What did the terms of reference for the Adani mine EIS require in reporting on economic matters? For a casual reader of the EIS this subject takes some finding.

If economic matters such as royalties paid to the owners of the coal are a primary consideration, at the very least on par with the major environmental ones, it could be expected that they would come early on in the terms of reference, and in the EIS. That is not the case as many pages in the terms of reference have to be turned (in fact, 74 pages) before reference is made to economic matters to be addressed in the EIS. And when we get there we are disappointed. The focus is narrow and hence of no utility in calculating whether or not the mine is justified in economic terms.

Of course, jobs do feature in the terms of reference. The governments and Adani's consultant could not have missed the media's unrelenting focus on jobs. Only occasionally will an informed commentator point out that mining creates few jobs and the preferred arrangement in the present era is for highly-paid workers to fly-in from a distant home base and fly-out when the shift is finished. When we come to the actual number to be employed by Adani be prepared for a surprise. The mayors of coastal or near coastal towns, such as Rockhampton, compete to be the home base of Adani workers. Share the number of mine workers around three towns and ponder the impact on each. Don't model it unless you have a top-class economist do it.

The economic matters referred to in the Adani EIS are local or regional in nature, and are modelled on assumptions that cannot be verified. The largest potential benefits of the mine, royalties to the State of Queensland and taxes to the Australian nation, deserve prominence yet do not get it. Job creation is given pride of place. The actual jobs created are not the 10,000, but a smidgeon. The big number was presumably a consequence of flawed modelling and/or inaccurate data fed into the model. We will never know the cause of the error due to a lack of transparency.

As already mentioned, it took challenges in the hearings of the Queensland Land Court to open up some of the basic economic issues that were glossed over in the EIS, and in some cases ignored. The truth was eventually established in a court where witnesses are expected to tell the truth and be examined on their evidence. Had this court not existed we may never have known that the jobs expected to be created are one-sixth of the number touted by the mining company and still boasted about by pro-Adani politicians. This part of the story is developed in more detail in due course.

There is no question that estimating royalty income, based as it is in Queensland on profits that we must expect will vary significantly over the years, is one of the most difficult matters to deal with in the economic assessment of a mining project. This difficulty also applies to Commonwealth taxes, for the same reason. However, these potential economic returns to the Queensland and Australian people are two of the most important factors if the mine is to be approved. If there is no reasonable expectation that worthwhile royalties and taxes are to be earned, everything else to do with the mine need not be considered. In other words, there is no point in wasting time and resources on a non-viable project. And there are no environmental issues to worry us if it is clear-cut that the mine fails on economic grounds.

One of the most important flaws in the EIS is the downplaying of royalty and tax estimates in the assessment of the mine. Why is this the case? The government's term of reference put it far down an extensive list. Maybe one should not give any credence to this. When we come to the matter in the terms of reference we find the requirement that: 'Potential impacts should consider local, regional state and national perspectives as appropriate to the scale of the project'. Here, one could expect that the most important potential benefits to the State and the Commonwealth, royalties and taxes, would have been the feature of the discussion. But no! How could an EIS be presented that did not deal with the major benefits of the project? A few jobs are insignificant in comparison to the potential payments to our governments. Having made this statement, I must admit that here I am envisaging a profitable mine. An assumption to go with the rest.

It is only at the very end of the 'Economies and management of impacts' section of the terms of reference for the EIS that there is reference to the need to formally deal with 'sustainable development'. It could be argued that sustainable development has been, since the late 1980s/early 1990s, the overarching framework for decision-making in Australia. It is not a brand-new concept that we are struggling to understand and implement.

The terms of reference recognise, if ever so briefly and broadly, the requirement of meeting *sustainable development* in terms of environmental, economic and social goals. This is stated in the following terms:

> Provide a comprehensive analysis of how the project conforms to the objectives for 'sustainable development'. (See the *National Strategy for Ecological Sustainable Development*.)
>
> This analysis should consider the cumulative impacts of the project (both beneficial and adverse) from a life-of-project perspective, taking into consideration the scale, intensity, duration and frequency of the impacts to demonstrate a balance between environmental integrity, social development and economic development. (Page 77 of the terms of reference.)

There are problems with such a vague statement of sustainable development. The fundamental principles of sustainable development are inter- and intra-generational equity, protecting biodiversity, the marriage of ecology and economics in decision-making at all levels, and the precautionary principle. Each is a yardstick that should have been applied in evaluating the Adani mine. The EIS and even the Land Court paid scant regard to most of these principles. The only two to exercise the minds of our decision-makers were biodiversity and the precautionary principle. Should our decision-makers be honest and state publicly that they are progressing to abandon the concept of sustainable development? This is probably unfair on them; however, they were taken on that route by the positive framing of the mine by Adani, successfully achieved.

That the Land Court did recognise the requirement to deal with sustainable development suggests that all is not lost on the recognition of its principles. That the treatment was cursory diminishes the accolade.

6

The confusion commences

Notwithstanding nearly eight years of formal assessment of the Adani mine it remains difficult to pin down its precise details. Whether this is deliberate or the result of an evolving business plan we have no idea. But what is very important is that a range of vastly different numbers on jobs, investment levels and time frames for the working-out of the mine have been reported.

There is no unambiguous set of figures (for example, workers employed, life of the mine, royalties paid to Queenslanders, company tax paid to the Australian Tax Office). This fact alone has provided ammunition for the project's opponents. Then when it comes to the offsets required of the mining company, we have some vague idea of what they are, but no evidence that they are feasible, and no understanding of what happens if they can't be met. Is there a Plan B if the offset ideas that are being mooted fail? We are not told that there is. Rather trust us.

Let us go back to the beginning in tracing through the mystery of the numbers. We start with the information provided by Adani to the Queensland government when it commenced its move to be allowed to mine. A document called an Initial Advice Statement was prepared and presented to the government. It was on the basis of the information in that document that the Queensland

Coordinator-General prepared the terms of reference for the Adani EIS.

In these terms of reference, up front in the very first paragraph, there is this extraordinary statement: 'The project has a potential mine life of 150 years.'

As George and Ira Gershwin sang about Methuseleh, who was supposed to have lived 969 years: 'It ain't necessarily so'.

By the time the EIS was submitted to the Queensland government the life of the mine had shrunk to 90 years. It was to continue shrinking. No explanations are to be found on the public record for the contracting timespan.

In the EIS we were told that 60 million tonnes of thermal coal will be mined per annum and the total mined over the mine's lifetime will be 7.8 billion tonnes. This is roughly accurate if the life of the mine is 90 years. However, Adani subsequently made yet another downward revision of the life of the mine to 60 years. On this basis the numbers on face value do not make sense. This you will discover is par for the course. If mining commenced in 2020 (the earliest it could) and the life-time was 90 years, mining would cease at the close of the first decade of the 22nd century, and even then restoration of the last areas mined would not be complete.

Note in passing that when the Adani economist gave evidence to the Land Court, using what seems on the face of it far superior modelling, he used a 40-year timeframe in his attempt to illustrate the economic performance of the mine. Let us not be too concerned with yet another statement of the mine's life. Keep in mind this is yet another modelling exercise.

Again, relying on the EIS, over the life-time of the mine the value of the investment is reported to be $21.5 billion. What is very important to note – a matter not publicised in the mainstream media – is that only a fraction of that amount is to be spent in the early years, with the remainder to be outlaid over the extremely long life of the mine (see below). Full production of coal is not anticipated until the tenth year of operation. The cost of production is estimated at $33 tonne. Rail transport from the mine to the port is reported to be $7.70 per tonne. These numbers are disputed in the Land Court hearings.

The total royalties and company tax to be paid are not reported in the EIS, rather there is a brief discussion of the royalty rate – a matter of no consequence without an estimate of the year-in, year-out profit of the mine.

Eventually, in the presentation of evidence to the Land Court hearing held after the EIS procedure had run its course, a royalty figure was given. Here, it should be noted that the Queensland government offered Adani a royalty 'holiday' to apply for the first two years of production. Why this would be necessary for a project that has to be deemed economically viable under Queensland mining law is yet another puzzle with no obvious answer.

As noted above, the total investment in the mine and railway was originally given at $21.5 billion. This is a lot of money. As will be reported later, since the EIS was submitted considerably less money is to be invested – another case of diminishing numbers. The $21.5 billion, or the smaller revised amount, would not be spent at once. It would, after the initial expenditure on infrastructure and equipment purchases, dwindle while reaching occasional highs as major mining equipment wears out and is replaced.

Recall, if Mr Adani obtains the finance he needs to commence mining, it will take 10 years for the mine to reach full production.

During these 10 years the total capital investment is stated to be $5.818 billion, or approximately 28% of the total investment over the life of the mine. This would mean that $15.7 billion would be spent over the remaining 80 years (but keep an eye on this number) of the life of the mine. If the expenditure was in equal amounts annually, which naturally it won't be but is used here for illustrative purposes, it would be only about $200 million per year. Putting that into context, this amount of money would buy in Australia between 200 to 300 houses each year. This is no large number.

Turning to employment, in particular jobs created. The Coordinator-General's terms of reference for the EIS suggests that there will be 5,000 in total during the construct phase at the mine site, on the rail line and at the port. When the mine is in full operation the number employed would be 4,000, according to the terms of reference. Both these estimates were provided to the Queensland government by Adani.

However, when the EIS was released these numbers had shrunk. At full production the number was stated to be 3,000. This would be built up over the first 10 years, from an initial 400 employees. After five years, the number of workers would be just over 2,000. Five years is a long wait for a keen entrepreneur seeking to reap benefits in local grocery sales. Then we are informed that over the lifetime of the mine, the average workforce would be 2,366 workers. This is a far call from the original claim of 10,000 jobs. Be prepared for yet another employment decrease when we come to the evidence given by an Adani representative to the Land Court.

A wide range of people, including the Prime Minister, have spoken of 10,000 jobs being created by the mine. Certainly, a rather impressive number for a capital-intensive industry. The fact that 10,000 is a false number seems not to have deterred some advocates for the mine from referring to it. We only discovered that it was a nonsensical result of an economic modelling exercise when the Adani economist was challenged in the Land Court hearings.

One can assume that the model was fed erroneous data in the first place and that some of the 'bells and whistles' in the model are prone to exaggerate both direct and indirect employment. Whatever the actual situation, the correction of this error, coming after the rather dramatic initial reduction in the life of the mine (from 150 years to 90, to 60 years), and the downward revision of the total investment to roughly three-quarters of Adani's original figure, $21.5 billion, should have alerted all interested parties – pro-mine, anti-mine and undecided – that much more serious investigation than the eight years of assessment had delivered to date was going to be needed to make sense of the Adani proposal. Blame no one but Adani for the drawn-out time period. Those who point to 'green tape' as the cause of delay, and assert that the Adani mine proposal has undergone a great amount of checking and hence should proceed immediately, have not read the evidence. They have not noticed the ever-changing Adani story. Had they taken notice, I guess they would be as unsure – even confused – as the average Australian is about the prospects that the mine would benefit the nation.

The hearings by the Land Court, held at the conclusion of the EIS process, opened up issues that had not been fully explored previously. At the conclusion of these hearings, the Adani mine did not appear to the clear-cut winner it had been touted to be for nearly a decade, or found to be in the EIS process. In fact, there was more uncertainty, more conflicting evidence than there ever had been. It is as if all the analysis in the draft, final and supplementary EISs had not taken place.

The last chapter is devoted to the court case. Before that there are other matters to explore.

7

Can we have our cake and eat it too?

What if the Adani mine is allowed to go ahead, can we compensate for the inevitable downside? The matter of compensating, other words offsetting, adverse impacts must be addressed because as I write the mine has made it through all formal barriers, with the exception of successfully offsetting the loss of habitat for the Black-throated Finch, the waxy cabbage palm, loss of Brigalow country, and some major water matters including the impact on some fabulous springs and associated billabongs. Never forget this is the country Banjo Paterson day-dreamed of as he worked away in his dingy Sydney office.

These on-site offset problems have been mentioned as the story has been developed and I shall come back to them in the next chapter. Before that, there are two so-far-ignored factors that must be explored in some detail. Both turn on the neglected principles of sustainable development.

Coal is in terms of human lifespans a finite resource. It was formed in the order of hundreds of millions of years ago. Keep digging it up and burning it and one day, relatively soon at the rate of mining at present, and all the relatively easy-to-mine deposits will be gone. There will be ever-more-costly-to-mine deposits, but when it costs more in fossil fuel energy to extract the coal than it can be sold for, it is no longer of use to us. It is no longer financially viable.

Let us not metaphorically bury coal, or more aptly leave it buried. Barbara Freese, a Minnesota lawyer, published in 2003 an excellent book titled *Coal: A Human History*. She writes (p. 10): 'Coal was no mere fuel, and no mere article of commerce. It represented humanity's triumph over nature – the foundation of civilization itself.'

She explains how coal provides us with light and power, with wealth and makes for a civilized lifestyle; darkness, weakness, poverty and barbarism no more. Putting aside one potentially civilization-destroying consequence of burning coal, Freese is correct. Today, as we approach the end of the coal age humanity faces a threat not experienced in historical terms. This is the climate-changing ability of a build-up of greenhouse gases in the atmosphere. Coal is one of the fossil fuel culprits. And a major one.

Without delaying the story, we will make abundantly clear that we are not ignorant of the dramatic climate changes that occurred in pre-historical times, as the climate-change deniers are prone to argue. Our knowledge is based on pre-written records. We know of the dramatic climatic episodes through the use of the most sophisticated measurement tools (for example, drilling into ice-cores). Based on our science we can describe with high degrees of certainty the thaw that raised sea-levels so high that Tasmania became separated from mainland Australia. This is but one example out of numerous ones, going as far far back as science takes us.

We will come to the issue of offsetting the environmental damage (climate change) caused by burning coal. But the first offsetting issue to deal with is what does the present generation do, burning coal as if it is a renewable resource, if it is morally obliged to hand over to future generations a world as productive as the one we live in? This is the sustainable development principle of inter-generational equity. It is given lip service in the Adani EIS and recognised by the Land Court but not pursued to the extent it requires. We do so here because it is very important while we continue to mine coal. It is important even if the Adani mine is never developed.

We know the coal resource is being depleted. We are reminded daily of the benefits we obtain from burning coal: electricity in the home, the lighting and air-conditioning in our palaces of commerce, the machinery in our factories. Take coal away and without a replacement source of power human society races to a bleak and brutish future. Of course, it is not just a matter of coal but also of natural gas and oil in its various forms.

The question is simple: How do we compensate our children and grandchildren if we have burned all the available coal and there is no alternative to provide electricity for their homes and work places? Yes, there are alternatives, but we are developing this scenario in their hypothetical absence to answer an issue of inter-generational equity, and point to what we should do with the resource rents and profits of mining coal. If the Adani mine is allowed to open and is profitable enough to pay royalties to the Queensland government and tax to the Commonwealth government, what should our governments do with this money?

Some might ask, do we have to compensate future generations if we use up all the coal? This is an ethical question, one which each person can answer on an individual basis. Nevertheless, it is a social issue – each one of us does not have his/her tiny coal mine and individual power plant. We need not concern ourselves with individual responsibility as some time ago now we dealt with the matter on a collective basis. The answer we came to goes by the principle of inter-generational equity (alternatively called 'inter-temporal equity'). This means nothing more or less than treating each generation equally. As you will recognise, this is not adhered to if an early generation uses up all the resources a future generation needs to be on par with the previous one. There is no problem if the present generation is, say, harvesting fish or felling timber. As long as each generation recognises its moral responsibility to future people, sustainable harvests can be estimated and taken. Obviously, we cannot do this with a finite resource such as coal. It is not possible to slow down the rate of burning coal, and other fossil fuels, so that these resources are available into the infinite future. Regardless of the rate of extraction, they must eventually run out.

The answer to the sustainability dilemma is that before we burn the last tonne of coal we need to have in place an alternative power source. There are two conflicting views on how this alternative source comes into being. First, there is a certain cadre of economists who will blithely say 'don't worry, the market will ensure that alternatives come on line as needed'. And, for good measure, they will add 'why concern ourselves with future generations as they are going to be better off than we are'. They base this proposition on the fact that year-in, year-out we in the industrialised countries have made enormous material progress. These economists measure progress in terms of GDP per capita, notwithstanding GDP's fundamental shortcomings. For non-economists we need to deal with this matter.

One example should suffice. In GDP terms, the greater the damage done by severe cyclones, hail storms, heat waves, droughts, coastal erosion and spread of disease – all features of global warming – the better off we are! We spend considerable money to replace the damaged property and deal with human health issues, and this money is added to our GDP!

While we know the serious limitations of the GDP measure, we have to admit – and admire – the progress we have made in the last 50 to 100 years. As a precursor to addressing the belief of the economic optimists, we need to recognise why they are that way inclined. Length of life is a standout indicator. At the end of the 20th century the average expected lifespan at birth of an Australian was approaching 85 years. At the beginning of the 20th century it was between 55 and 60 years, depending on gender, a thirtyish year difference. We do not doubt the ability of our medical scientists and specialists to keep advancing medicine. We have goods and services at unbelievable cheap prices, due in the main to the economic and technological revolution in China – the globe's cheap factory. These and other indicators would have us believe that our children and grand-children will be better off than we are – possibly much better off. However, ...

In coming to a rosy conclusion about the future we are neglecting the potential serious adverse impacts of climate change. If the impacts are as serious as the official predictions indicate, the near-future generations and those that follow will be worse off.

The question we should address is: How do we compensate for the fact that we – selfishly – have used up all the fossil fuels? Here we introduce the Hartwick Rule. In plain English this rule states that if a nation's income is going to be sustained through time at its present level, sustaining incomes is the means by which we sustain our healthy and wealthy lifestyles. There is the need to replace depleted 'natural capital' such as a coal body with another capital asset capable of earning the same level of income. This means that profits plus resource rents earned from the exploitation of coal have to be invested in other economic pursuits capable of earning the same level of income as coal mining did. This is the Hartwick Rule from the name of the economist who formulated it.

It could be argued that given the unique nature of coal – it drives much of the modern economy – the investment should be in direct replacements to coal-fired power stations, the obvious large-scale candidates being hydro-electricity schemes, including pumped-storage hydro, nuclear power (fission), wind turbines, geothermal power systems and large-scale solar farms, not to overlook the popular individual roof-top solar panels. Other energy sources could eventuate, in particular, nuclear fusion and hydrogen-based energy, but they remain firmly stuck on the drawing board rather than knocking on the door.

Events in the real world suggest that there is no need to use the profits from coal, gas or oil as investments in renewable energy sources. The latter are standing on their own feet. Wind power is as cheap, if not cheaper, than electricity generated by coal. Solar farms are benefitting from scale economies and are close to being on par with coal-fired electricity. Pumped storage hydro-electricity compensates for the intermittency of wind and solar and has enormous potential. We can expect that the renewable energy sector will displace the fossil-fuel-derived stationary energy sector in the foreseeable future. As a consequence, the profits obtained from mining and burning fossil fuels can be invested in a wide portfolio. Of this we have real world examples. One sticks out. We let Paul Cleary, a senior writer for the *Australian* newspaper, tell the story.

Cleary commences by comparing Australia to Norway and explains the relevance by the fact that these countries are number one and two on the United Nations Human Development Index. Norway pips Australia. Mother Nature has been very kind to both countries. Norway has oil to export. Australia has coal to export.

Cleary (*Too Much Luck: The Mining Boom and Australia's Future*, 2011, p. 64) writes:

> a combination of resource wealth and first-world institutions has proved to be the sweet spot, evaluating quality of life in the two countries to the maximum available. But Norway differs from Australian in one very important way – it is certain to remain in its enviable position long after the resources have been depleted. Australia has no such certainty.

> Norway ... has ... had great leadership, including that of former Prime Minister Gro Harlem Brundtland. Brundtland articulated the concepts of sustainable development and inter-generational equity – the idea that the current generation should not leave future generations worse off ... Taking on board the principles of inter-generational equity, [the Norwegians] set up a petroleum fund that is as breathtaking as it is simple in design and purpose. In essence, Norway's fund transforms a non-renewable resource into a financial asset that can last for ever. It does this through the principle that no more than ... 4% of the fund should be spent in any one year.

There are other important features of this sovereign wealth fund, to call it by its formal, generic name. A very important one is that the oil profits are not invested in Norway but rather overseas. As a consequence there is no inflationary impact in Norway. Another feature is that investment is not permitted in ethically unsound industries. The businesses that have been 'blacklisted' include Wal-Mart, Rio Tinto, Thales and Seco (which operates detention centres in Australia).

Norway's sovereign wealth fund is boosted by government majority ownership of its oil, and an additional tax on oil production. When Cleary published his book in 2011, the extra tax was set at 50 percent on the normal corporate tax rate. To quote Cleary (p. 66) this is 'for the privilege of profiting from the wealth of Norwegians'.

While one can read in newspapers and hear on talk-back radio and current affairs television programs calls by Australians to introduce a sovereign wealth fund and to take an ownership position with regard to the underground resources that Australians already own, our governments have no stomach for what are economically and ethically justified actions. Cleary (p. 71) found that economists in the Commonwealth Treasury had 'a curious bias against sovereign wealth funds'.

I can't help think that if Australian governments, both Commonwealth and State/Territory, were today sitting on a substantial sovereign wealth fund, built-up over the numerous mining booms we have experienced since the 1960s, as voters we would be far less critical of mining proposals. I realise this idea would not suit the miners, as resource rents and profits would be contributions to the fund. Our Commonwealth government attempted to introduce a resource rent tax, and we witnessed the opposition to it. The miners won.

The power of the mining lobby and the media that supports it is simply too strong. On this issue prime ministers are removed without testing the will of the people in an election. That there is very significant foreign ownership of mining and energy businesses is conveniently overlooked. Where do the profits go? From where is the mine machinery imported? As Cleary (p. 87) states: 'Trying to establish just how much money the [mining] industry makes is no longer as straightforward as it once was.' Notwithstanding that difficulty, Cleary (p. 83) makes the point that 'taxes and royalties haven't kept up with the huge profits now being earned'.

We should note here that two journalists for the *Weekend Australian* (10–11 February 2018), in a long article which is supportive of the Adani mine, wrote: 'Part of the problem with Adani … is that its finances and decision-making processes are not only opaque, but far removed.' My perspective is that this is a very large part of the problem.

If we as a nation were serious about gaining as much money as possible from our underground resources, the obvious solution would be for Australian governments to retain ownership of coal and the other resources and invite mining companies to tender for the job of mining the resources, offering them a realistic return for their effort. Notwithstanding that this is a normal business deal in a capitalist economy, some would condemn this as 'socialism', completely overlooking the fact that as owners of the resources we can do what we like with them. The perverse nature of Australian politics would turn such an idea into a diabolical ideological struggle.

Even the case made by Cleary to introduce a sovereign

wealth fund in Australia is likely to be lambasted as 'socialism', notwithstanding that the concept is supported by a number of far-sighted Liberal Party politicians including the present Prime Minister, Malcolm Turnbull. Returning to the Norwegian case, which is supported by Cleary, it is significant that the sovereign wealth fund was introduced by a conservative government.

In summary, there would seem to be no prospect that in the foreseeable future Australian governments will concern themselves with offsetting the depletion of non-renewable resources. This applies to the proposed Adani mine. Quite how Australian governments expect to meet the inter-generational equity principle to which they have signed up to is not at all clear from their behaviour with regard to coal, iron ore and other resources.

To the next major offset problem.

The burning of the coal mined by the Adani will produce a considerable amount of carbon dioxide. Various estimates are reported. According to Adani it would be 4.8 billion tonnes. One estimate that gets considerable air-play (based on calculations made by the Australia Institute) suggests that the Adani coal when burned will create annual emissions of a similar order of magnitude to those of countries such as Malaysia and Austria, more than Bangladesh and Sri Lanka, and only marginally less than Vietnam.

We know that the Adani coal will fire power stations in India. These power stations and the ultimate consumer, electricity-using households and businesses in India, are responsible for the greenhouse gases according to international protocols. Opponents to the mine argue it matters not where the emissions occur. Their case hinges on an interpretation of definitions in the *EPBC Act*. For example, is the definition of the 'environment' broad enough to apply to the global environment? Or what is basically the same question, is the 'planetary ecosystem' (the globe) consistent with the definition in Section 528 of the Act?

Social, economic and cultural matters are defined as part, or aspects, of the environment. In as much as we live in a global economy – of this we are reminded by our politicians and our media outlets – economic matters are increasingly global in nature. One can appreciate the case that is made by those who trace through the mining of Adani's coal – being burned in India – to the impact additional greenhouse gases will have on the health of the Great Barrier Reef. One can also appreciate the complexity and resultant difficulty involved dealing with such matters in a world of sovereign nation states – notwithstanding the existence of United Nations and notions of a global community.

We have to deal with political reality which means the strength of nationalism, in contrast to real world economics.

Notwithstanding what Australian law might or might not say about the boundaries of 'the environment', international protocols require emissions to be counted in the country where they occur. This is the polluter-pays principle in operation. In climate change jargon, these emissions are called 'scope 3' emissions. Those making the case against the Adani mine argue that its contribution to climate change will be disastrous for the health of the Great Barrier Reef. Professor Ove Hoegh-Guldberg (2015) was asked to address this matter. In summary he found that:

> As we are already above the thermal threshold for damage to reef building corals and hence coral reefs, any further

addition of CO_2 into the atmosphere will directly damage the Great Barrier Reef ... The true cost of the emitted carbon from the Carmichael Mine to the Great Barrier Reef and other ecosystems, businesses and human health must be calculated and attached to any decision on whether or not to proceed with the mine. To ignore the impact of the mine, knowing that the emissions from the extracted coal are not going to be sequestered, ignores the much greater costs of the mine to people and businesses worldwide.

Hoegh-Gulberg is correct in stating that there is no proposal to offset the extra greenhouse gases in the atmosphere resulting from burning the Adani coal. We should note in passing that sequestering is used to describe two radically different processes. The usual process, the one promoted to airline passengers, is to grow trees. Airline passengers can make a voluntary contribution of some dollars to an organisation which undertakes to plant trees. Growing trees take in carbon dioxide and store it in the trees and the soil. Trees and all matter of living things became coal. But, trees planted today decay and in the process release CO_2. Hundreds of millions of years would have to pass before the decayed trees became coal. That noted, Adani is not going to plant trees to sequester the CO_2 emitted from the Indian power stations.

The other method of sequestration will, if it becomes economically viable, entail capturing carbon dioxide as it comes out of the power station and transporting it to a disposal site where it will be stored permanently. Various homes for the CO_2 have been suggested, including abandoned coal mines and the deep ocean. The evidence to date suggests that this form of carbon sequestration is likely to be technically feasible, immensely costly and probably decades away. By then the coal age could have ended.

In summary, as matters stand, the question of offsetting the increased greenhouse gas emissions from burning coal produced in the Adani mine has been raised, but if anything is to be done in this regard it will have to be done in India and paid for by Adani, or more likely those who purchase the Adani coal.

8

Are offsets mirages on the outback track to the Adani mine?

In this chapter we explore the application of direct offsets in the Adani case, that is, how do we compensate for the loss of Black-throated Finch habitat? How do we compensate for loss of clumps of waxy cabbage palm? Or of Brigalow country? How do we ensure that local farmers are not forced to drill ever further down for water – to the Devil in Banjo Paterson's words – as their bores dry up because water is being taken by the mine?

If not offsets, what? We have looked to them in hope. But the evidence is mounting to suggest that we have been far too optimistic.

Are environmental offsets a sop or a solution? Much effort is put into developing offsets that in a perfect world would deliver what they are designed to do. Public servants and individual scientists beaver away in this work. Environmental advocates have, until the Adani case, been relatively relaxed, trusting in the offset concept. The public has put its faith – trust – in the scientists and public servants and, for better or worse, the law-makers who have told us that they have found the solution to our environmental concerns.

It will take no more than one, widely-reported, flawed case to destroy that trust, and environmental management will regress to the pitiful days of the 1960s.

What is the point of approving projects, such as the Adani mine, before offsets have been formulated in sufficient detail for us to have a justified belief that they will save the birds, the palms and the bush? Offsets that are designed *after* the mine has been approved – as is the case we are about to face – could fail to deliver. They could be inappropriate. They could be impossible to put into practice.

I am not the first to identify this major flaw in the application of offsets. A Senate inquiry into environmental offsets in 2014 (Senate Standing Committee on Environment and Communications: 'Environmental Offsets') heard witness after witness argue that approvals for major projects, such as coal mines, were being given prior to offsets being fully developed and secured. A clear statement of the failure is enunciated by a witness to the Senate inquiry who stated that granting of approvals prior to securing offsets is a 'systematic and repeated failure of offset policy'. The available evidence, and the Adani case, indicates this situation has not changed over the past four years.

Why not make approval of the mine conditional on proven offsets, not vague promises that will become vague plans and strategies and, then, what happens if they fail? If this is the result of the Adani mine case and the Black-throated Finch population declines dramatically, will a government close down the mine?

To be fair to Adani, a long list of 'commitments' to undertake a wide range of activities, including providing offsets, was published with the Coordinator-General's evaluation of the former's EIS; however, the commitments remain very vague. With regard to the Black-throated Finch the report states (Appendix 7):

The loss of habitat ... will occur in stages ... Management actions to encourage the dispersal away from areas that will be cleared ... will ... be developed. Management actions ... will seek to maintain and where possible enhance habitats and populations (e.g. through pest control, provision of water sources, appropriate grazing and fire management) ... in offset areas. Important population, movement and habitat information ... will be collected, particularly with respect to seasonal use, key areas, nest sites, important feeding areas and management of threatening processes.

More recently the Biodiversity Offsets Strategy (BOS) was prepared. The most important data and discussion have been redacted. In summary, the EIS and BOS show how little was/ is known about the Black-throated Finch and the prospects of saving it. These documents provide no justification to approve the mine.

Is it the case that with the Adani mine we are witnessing a rush to a decision? Have the pro-mine advocates spooked the waivering politicians into supporting the mine while very serious doubts remain about not only the touted economic benefits, but the miner's ability to do no harm at the local scale? It is noteworthy that after a near decade of governments assessing the Adani mine, there seems to be a lack of willingness to wait until workable offsets are formulated and put in place.

To ask Adani to formulate scientifically-proven offset proposals – including cementing formal agreements with landholders – is little to ask, particularly given that Mr Adani is in no hurry to start mining. Be mindful that if Mr Adani was keen to commence mining he has had the approval of both the Commonwealth and Queensland governments since the Land Court of Queensland handed down its findings in 2015. If his original plans to mine had been fulfilled, mining would have commenced in 2014 – obviously he would have had to wait until the decision by the Land Court which came one year later. Adani has had much time to sort out a detailed offset plan. Both the Commonwealth and the Queensland governments could have waited to approve or not approve the mine without causing any financial harm to Adani.

Under the Queensland offset law and policy, there is a requirement to undertake an 'ecological equivalence assessment' as a precursor to formulating offsets. This is a simple, two-part ecological exercise involving fieldwork and some remote sensing. The method is that the environment and the flora and fauna in it that will be adversely affected – destroyed where the open-cut mining takes place – are studied and the results used to identify similar environments that can act as offsets. The second part of the study is to undertake a science-based study of potential substitute environments. In the type of project we are discussing, these substitutes are likely to be adjoining or, at least nearby, the impacted area. What we find in the Adani case is that the first part of the procedure has been done – in 2014 – while we still wait for the second part.

Do we want to continue to rely on the philosophy of environmental offsets? If we do, the Adani case is going to be a make or break case. Let us go to the detail.

The concept of compensating projects was developed in recognition that humans caused, regardless of intent or not, adverse environmental impacts, but also had, in the appropriate circumstances, the ability to do things which neutralised them. Offsets came into being as the likely saviour of modern lifestyles. If they fail us, there will be great loss of confidence in environmental management – and trust in the decision-makers who sold us on the potential value of offsets.

The Commonwealth Government via its Department of the Environment has an offsets policy related to the *EPBC Act*. The problem is that the offset policy is not law – we cannot seek a legal means to challenge a decision-maker, a minister of the Crown, to impose adequate, workable offsets. That stated, see below for the suggestion that there could be a possible opening in law. The Commonwealth government also has an offset evaluation framework to be used by its public servants who are tasked with assessing the offsets that are proposed by those who have to put them in place.

In terms of the Adani mine, the Department of the Environment has produced a pamphlet titled *Carmichael Coal Mine Project – Frequently Asked Questions* (n.d.). In this it makes the reliance on offsets an explicit requirement before mining is allowed:

> Where impacts could not [*sic*] be avoided, offsets are required to compensate. Importantly, a detailed Biodiversity Offset Strategy is required of the proponent for approval by the Minister for the Environment before mining can commence. At a minimum the offsets must include – protection and improvement of 31,000 hectares of southern black-throated finch habitat.

Before addressing matters of terminology in the above quote, I need to point out that the Queensland Coordinator-General refers to 16,500 hectares of Black-throated Finch habitat that would be adversely impacted. Maybe the Commonwealth and Queensland governments are referring to different things – or maybe this is just another case of inconsistency, a matter of major concern throughout the Adani case.

The following words in the quote above need careful

consideration. The words that could become the subject of debate are 'detailed', 'protection' and 'improvement'.

In another Commonwealth Government document, this one titled *Offsets under National Law* there are words that help determine what 'detailed' means. We are informed that offsets are to be 'timely, transparent, scientifically robust and reasonable'. With regard to transparency the requirement is to 'have transparent governance arrangements including being able to be readily measured, monitored, audited and enforced'. These words need no definition. An interested person should be able to identify on a map – and more importantly on the ground – the precise area/areas that are subject to protection and improvement and contemplate via on-ground inspection the manner by which the offset will be delivered.

If this were to be the case, it would be a radical improvement on the lack of information in Adani's *Environmental Offset Package Carmichael Coal Mine and Rail Project*. In this consultant-produced report – any shortcomings should not be attributed to the consultant, rather Adani – five grazing properties adjacent to the mine that are deemed suitable to offset adverse impacts on Brigalow, the Black-throated Finch and waxy cabbage palms are listed as 'Property 1, 2, 3, 4 and 5'. Why can't the properties be named so that an interested person could, if nothing else, do a computer search of the vegetation, availability of water holes and the size of the cattle herd? These variables would allow for an initial appreciation of the suitability of the area, before ground-truthing took place. No such detail is given. In fact, no detail, only numbers as property names.

Presumably, it was on this consultant's report that the Commonwealth Minister for the Environment approved the mine.

The Queensland government provides for public scrutiny a list of all offsets approved by it. The Commonwealth government has been promising for at least four years to list the offsets it approves, but a list does not exist. In the Adani case both governments would list the same offsets as a condition of the 'one-stop-shop' environmental impact assessment agreement between the two levels of government. If I cannot find a list of approved offsets for the Adani mine, I would suggest no one else can.

In the document *Offsets under National Law* we are told that offsets have to be approved under the *EPBC Act*. However, it would seem to be the case that the Commonwealth minister was able to approve the Adani mine before a biodiversity offset strategy was prepared and submitted to him. As of the time of writing, February 2018, there is no public evidence that appropriate, secured offsets exist. If this is the case, it runs counter to what the public is told in *Offsets under National Law*, where it is stated that: 'The suitability of a proposed offset is considered part of the decision to approve or not approve a proposed action under the *EPBC Act*.'

We are told that Commonwealth minister will assess and make a decision on an offset strategy *before mining commences*. Under the EPBC Act's offsets assessment guide, Adani would have to submit an offset management plan to the minister three months prior to the commencement of mining. Recall, this minister has already approved the mine. What does he do if the offset proposal is not satisfactory and, given the specific requirements of the Black-throated Finch (its habitat, water holes, preferred grass seeds), it proves impossible to protect a sustainable population of the bird?

This takes us back to the *Frequently Asked Questions* document.

An area of 31,000 hectares of suitable land has to be *protected* for the survival of the finch. What does 'protected' mean in this case? On this subject it is extremely important that an offset cannot be claimed where under existing law the purpose of the offset is already being achieved. The Queensland government's offset policy and law (*Environmental Offsets Act 2014*) makes it clear that an offset must provide *additional protection* to that already in existence. The matter of *additionality* was discussed in some detail in the senate inquiry in 2014. In evidence to this inquiry, this principle was recognised by the Commonwealth public servants as fundamental to the concept of offsetting. Additionality is central to the accounting of greenhouse gas offsetting, and is recognised as equally important in more general environmental offsetting.

Let us consider the land that surrounds the proposed mine, part of which is in the property acquired by Adani and the remainder in the grazing properties identified by numbers by Adani, although they are known by their names by all others. These are grazing properties with significant patches of habitat deemed suitable for the Black-throated Finch. If this land were to be used for offsetting, providing substitute habitat for the finches, it would have to be protected from clearing among other requirements.

However, it may be that this land is already subject to restrictions on clearing of finch habitat, meaning that the offset would not meet the principle of additionality. In asserting that the land could not be legally cleared two fundamental factors come into play. First, the Black-throated Finch is listed as endangered under the Queensland *Nature Conservation Act 1992*. This means that if Black-throated Finches already live in the land in question (or other parts of the 31,000 hectares of potential habitat), the destruction of this habitat may require a permit and assessment under the *Nature Conservation Act*. If the finch does not already live on this habitat, the question must be asked as to why not? Experts in giving evidence in the Land Court have admitted that there is a high level of uncertainty as to why the Black-throated Finch prefers the habitat on the Adani mine site, making any attempt at providing an offset for this habitat questionable without explaining this. Then there is the Queensland *Vegetation Management Act 1999*, which may also provide additional restrictions around clearing land, regardless of the existence of the finch.

My interpretation could be flawed. I say this because Adani's consultant on offsets comments that land which presently supports Black-throated Finches could become an offset, under certain conditions: 'Offset areas for black-throated finch which already contain the species will need to demonstrate improvement of finch conservation outcomes through specific management improvements or decreased threats'.

This suggests that it would be possible to improve the existing habitat to the extent that it could sustain a larger Black-throated Finch population; that is, allowing finches displaced due to loss of habitat from land-clearing for the mine to permanently settle in the improved area. In this hypothetical case, improvement could entail reducing feral animals, such as pigs, regenerating and rehabilitating the land to create new habitat, or creating artificial watering holes.

The concept of 'like-for-like' comes into play in settling on an offset solution. Clearly, some natural attributes are unique, irreplaceable, not able to be recreated. However, this is not necessarily the case for the Black-throated Finch. Just as humans can change homes – as long as the features they require are provided – so can many other animals. We simply do not know in the case of the finch. That noted, there are other matters that could frustrate the movement of a bird population to a new, even if nearby, home. These are discussed later.

I noted above the Adani consultant's proposition that areas where the Black-throated Finch already lives could be improved. If successful, such action is likely to increase the local population of the finch. That itself could stop any forced migration of finches from habitat destroyed by the mine. Any habitat has a maximum carrying capacity. It is possible that this is the case for the suggested offset areas. We simply don't know.

Nevertheless, if the finch population in total increases, this improvement would be recorded as an offset. From a biological and evolutionary point of view, it is the maintenance of a viable population of the Black-throated Finch that matters, not individual birds.

As for the Black-throated Finch, so for the plant and plant community that have to be protected – or workable offsets put in place – the waxy cabbage palm and the remaining Brigalow country. We are waiting! These three come under the category of 'Matters of National Environmental Significance' in the *EPBC Act*, a status that means workable offset solutions have to be found.

The issue of water used by the mine is in the hands of both the Queensland and Commonwealth governments. Much debate took place in the Land Court hearings on the possible/probable adverse impact on graziers and ecosystems resulting from the dewatering process, which is a necessity for coal mining in the area. Under the Queensland *Water Act 2000* the department managing water allocation and use has the power to ensure that in granting a licence for mine dewatering 'make good' provisions are in place. The Queensland Coordinator-General has recommended that, prior to mining, but subsequent to his approval of the mine, 'the proponent must develop a detailed plan to guarantee the long-term security of water for all current groundwater users predicted to be affected by the project' (COG, 2014, p. xiv).

The Coordinator-General noted that Adani has committed to 'make good' all impacts on landowner water supplies. There are various options to 'make good', including deepening a bore or otherwise improving a bore's capacity, drilling new bores or otherwise providing an alternative water supply. Monetary compensation is another option; however, this would run counter to the long-term economic sustainability of a grazing property.

The Commonwealth government's requirement is that a groundwater plan be prepared and approved by the Minister for the Environment before mining can commence. Furthermore, a certain quantity of water has to be returned to the Great Artesian Basin within a five-year time-span. We have no details. Next, I will point to a potentially important legal case.

In 2013, an environmental organisation, the Northern Inland Council for the Environment, undertook a legal challenge in the Federal Court of Australia against the Commonwealth Minister for the Environment for having granted approval to clear vegetation to allow coal mining without having approved offsets. Justice Cowdrey said that he understood that this was detrimental to the environment, but the law permitted it (*Northern Inland Council for the Environment* v. *Minister for the Environment 2013*). The judge commented: 'It is correct … that offset conditions need not be satisfied prior to commencing approved clearing'.

Is this the best we can hope for until the law is changed? Possibly, the judge's view of the law could be found to be wrong. This is not for me to speculate on. I'm not a lawyer.

Some hope is found in the opinion by environmental lawyer Sue Higginson in her evidence to the Senate inquiry into environmental offsets. She argued that there is a provision in the *EPBC Act* that would allow revoking a formally approved development, if damage was done but offsets had not been approved. The appropriate section of the *EPBC Act* is section 145. In lay language, if new information of environmental harm becomes available the minister can revoke the approval, so long as that information is of a kind that would have led the minister to refuse approval at the outset.

This legal proposition could come to play a make-or-break role for the Adani mine.

9

You be the judge

This chapter is the most difficult to write – simply because I shall be criticising the findings of a highly respectable legal person, none other than the President of the Land Court of Queensland. Of course, no one in a democracy should be above criticism; but given the difficult and, I assume, lonely work of judicial officers they deserve praise for their efforts, not criticism. The Land Court President whom I take to task is Carmel MacDonald. She has retired since the Adani case.

The Adani case is formally *Adani Ming Pty Ltd v Land Services of Coast and Country Inc & Ors [2015] QLC48).* The handing down of the findings and recommendations occurred on 15 December 2015.

As noted previously, the Land Court hearings followed the lengthy period over which the environmental impact assessment took place. The environmental group going by the lengthy title Land Services of Coast and Country Inc lodged its objections to the granting of the Adani mining leases and the 'draft environmental authority' on 1 October 2014.

Recall that earlier that year both the Queensland Coordinator-General and Commonwealth Environment Minister had approved the mine. On 7 May, the Queensland Coordinator-General released his evaluation of the Adani EIS. He recommended approval of the mine 'subject to conditions and recommendations'. Next, on 24 July 2014, the Commonwealth government approved the project 'subject to conditions'; although it was forced by legal action to withdraw this approval, but soon had a new one reworked and the mine and rail-line were finally given the go-ahead on 14 October 2014. One other governmental requirement was needed and that was a draft environmental authority from the Queensland government under the Queensland *Environment Protection Act 1994*. That was provided on 28 August 2014.

After the public release of the two Queensland government documents, interested parties had the right to challenge in the Land Court of Queensland. As noted above, objections were lodged at the beginning of October that year. The objections were to the granting of three coal-mining leases to Adani under the *Mineral Resources Act 1989* and the formal approval of Adani's draft environmental authority by the Queensland Department of Environment and Heritage Protection, exercising power under section 186(a) of the *Environmental Protection Act*.

I'll come to the grounds for objection, but a few words on the Land Court are warranted. It is in its own words a 'specialised judicial tribunal and court of record'. The court evolved from a very old Queensland court which was established in 1898 to deal with Crown leasehold land, a fraught matter as the outback was being opened up. Until 2007, the Land Court had no role in mining matters, but when the Land and Resources Tribunal was effectively abolished and its powers given to the Land Court, mining matters became a core judicial matter of the latter. Go back to before the formation of the Land and Resources Tribunal and mining matters in Queensland that from an environmental perspective were objections on *public interest* grounds were heard by local Mining Wardens (usually local Magistrates). Both the Tribunal and the Land Court are vast improvements on the Mining Wardens' hearings.

It is necessary before continuing with the Land Court story to make known that with regard to mining matters its power is to make recommendations to the Queensland minister responsible for mining; that is, the court is not the final arbitrator. Whether or not a mine is approved in Queensland is a political matter, a judgement of the Queensland Cabinet, with the caveat that if the Commonwealth government has a responsibility, as there is in the Adani case, the approval of a mine is determined by both governments; or only one, the Commonwealth, if the mined resource is to be exported. There is a famous case in the mid-1970s when the Commonwealth government effectively closed down mining on Fraser Island by refusing to grant export permits. The Queensland government was more than happy to see mining continue but without sales overseas there was no point to mining. This is how Fraser Island was pretty much left intact and became a World Heritage Area.

There are two matters which must be noted about the Land Court, particularly when it hears extremely complex matters. The Adani case is of that nature. One matter bears on the knowledge held by those who sit in judgement. When the issue is the functioning of artesian water, springs, lagoons and the comparatively simple-to-comprehend flow of rivers, in-depth knowledge of a large number of disciplines is a necessity. When it comes to questions of zoology, biology and ecology that determine the sustainable population of the Black-throated Finch, no generalist environmental scientist, let alone someone expert in an unrelated discipline, has a chance to answer the questions. When it comes to the costs and benefits of mining and the use of coal, only expert economists have the tools and understanding of their limitations to come to a professional judgement.

It is unfair and unreasonable to expect a lawyer, without recourse to expert advisers present at the hearings, to listen to complex, often disputed matters between opposing experts, and come to an evidence-based finding on the facts.

The other matter, trivial in importance, is that the President of the Land Court and the other statutory appointments are called 'Members' not judges. I note this to explain why I am not using the title 'Judge'.

It will be clear from what I written above that while Members of the Land Court are highly qualified and skilled lawyers, they are not scientists or economists. One cannot expect them to have much more than lay knowledge of complex environmental and economic matters. I understand that this problem has been identified as such and the new President of the Land Court, Fleur Kingham, was chosen because she has a long professional history in dealing with environmental issues; and given the likelihood of many more complex mining cases being brought to the court, she has a professional history in this sector of the Queensland economy. President Kingham is unique in this regard as well as others.

To return to the Adani hearings that took place in 2015, the then President of the court found herself having to grapple with some of the most complex scientific and economic matters. In a hearing like the Adani one, there will normally be two sets of experts appearing before the court, one representing the prospective miner and the other representing those objecting to the mine.

To assist the court, a procedure exists where the experts from both sides are asked to come together and confer. The result of this process will be a report to the court, called a 'joint report', containing statements on all matters agreed. For example, in the Adani hearings the opposing sides agreed that the present state of global warming (climate change) was caused by us, humans. Nothing surprising here, except that some of the most strident promoters of the Adani mine are climate change deniers.

Joint reports are a good idea. But only so much is normally agreed via this process. Therefore, to facilitate exploration of contested issues, individual reports are allowed to be prepared and submitted to the court. As a general rule, it is the conflicting evidence which is the most complex – and on this we must empathise with Members of the court.

It is time to delve deeper into the Adani hearings. The President of the Land Court delivered her findings and recommendations (in legal jargon her 'orders') on 15 December 2015. Her findings and recommendations run to 139 pages.

The first major issue deals with the allocation, use and depletion of water on and around the proposed mine site. To illustrate how important – and how difficult – this issue is, the President used over 50 pages of her 139 pages of findings and recommendations deliberating on water issues. I would require another book to explain in any detail the matters aired, some agreed, many challenged, and at the end of the day the fundamental ones not reconciled.

It was not the case that the President of the court would leave unreconciled these conflicts. She had confidence in her ability to pick the winner. I tried that task out on myself – given that I have some knowledge of water matters from my professional work, and that I understand from experience the responsibilities and challenges of 'sitting in judgement' on highly technical matters. In a previous professional appointment I had one very similar to the President, when I was a Commissioner of the Industry Commission from 1990 to 1996. Public hearings on significant economic matters were the Commission's bread and butter.

After reading and re-reading the various reports on water-related issues that were tendered to the court, reading a number of times the President's deliberations, I admitted defeat. If I was asked to make a finding it would be that the experts go back into the field and get more data. If they still could not agree, let their data be examined by a panel of their peers. There is an analogy to this in important medical matters. I am a strong advocate of obtaining the advice from three medical specialists. I tell my students that this is a sound principle which could be applied across disciplines.

One way of illustrating the vast range of specialist expertise that would be needed to arrive at an evidence-based conclusion on the questions pertaining to water in the Adani case, is the large number of water-related disciplines that were referred to in the hearings. Here is the list: hydrology, hydraulics, hydrogeology, hydrochemistry, geochemistry, geology, stratigraphy, lithology and geomorphology.

That the President of the court found that she could navigate her way around, and between, the theory and practice of these disciplines is truly noteworthy. She has much more confidence than I do. In coming to her conclusions she placed great faith in the *promises* that various offsets and the untried practises of *adaptive management* could deliver environmentally appropriate results.

What in a nutshell were/are the water debates about? A

critical argument by those opposing the mine is that ecologically valuable groundwater-dependent springs will be severely impacted. One group of these springs goes by the name of the Doongmabulla Springs Complex. Whoever named the individual springs obviously knew a bit of the Bible. We get Moses Spring, Little Moses Spring and Joshua. Maybe it was the preacher who christened Michael Magee's son 'Maginnis' after the bottle of Maginnis whiskey the preacher carried. Or maybe it is because the springs are considered to be one million years old that Biblical thoughts came to mind. Whatever the case, if you are not familiar with Banjo Paterson's 'A Bush Christening' I can recommend it. There is also the Mellaluka Springs Complex, comprising Mellaluka Spring, Lignum Spring and Stories Spring. These are not as ecologically important.

The Doongmabulla Springs complex comprises large, permanent springs that supply water in a continuous flow to the Upper Carmichael River, which flows into the Carmichael River. These springs support vegetation of high ecological value. The springs are only eight kilometres to the west of the proposed mine. The major concern is that the extensive dewatering necessary in the mining process could cause these springs to stop flowing, in fact to disappear.

All the water and earth sciences that I listed above were brought to bear as the pro- and anti-mining experts argued before the Land Court. The President of the court was inclined to favour the pro-mining arguments, while noting that there had been a lack of modelling undertaken by the Adani experts. She said 'I consider that a lack of direct investigation or modelling is concerning'.

Read on further in her report and the President comments 'There is evidence supporting both parties' position'; but she came to favour the pro-mining argument while remaining doubtful. She commented that 'the lack of investigation and modelling … has raised some doubt in my mind as to [my pro-mining] conclusion'. But obviously the doubts were not strong enough.

These few quotes from the President's findings suggest a fair degree of uncertainty on her behalf. As her conclusions indicate, she puts great faith in research that has not been done and in a 'Groundwater Dependent Ecosystem Management Plan' that also has not been produced. This plan has to be approved by the Queensland Department of Environment and Heritage Protection. Under the Commonwealth *EPBC Act*, another research *plan* – not research results – has to be approved at least three months prior to the start of excavations. Furthermore, the President commented 'While I accept the evidence that if the Springs run dry the ecological community will be lost and that loss cannot be effectively offset, I consider that the conditions in both the draft environmental authority and the *EPBC Act* approval are … appropriate for mitigating the risk of threat to the ecological value of the springs.'

In terms of offsetting the destruction of the springs, if destruction was the result, the idea was put to the court that springs 'in other locations' be investigated and if degraded they could be (somehow) re-established. This concept was opposed on the grounds that this was not a 'like-for-like' offset, and it was not possible to reconstruct the hydrological, biological and chemical conditions in an artificial situation. As noted above, on this matter the President sided with the opponents to the mine. That stated, it can only be concluded that *post-approval* processes are the rule, not the exception, in the Adani case. There are more of them to come.

Turning attention to the fate of the Waxy Cabbage Palm, there was agreement between the opposing experts that it is a very rare plant, that the Carmichael River population is 'the most globally significant population of this species ... The species is vulnerable and the Carmichael River population is considered necessary for the species long-term survival'. The rival experts agreed that the palms required reliable flows of water and adequate levels of soil moisture. They also agreed that the distribution of the palms and their relationship between hydrology are subjects needing further study.

Agreement was not to go beyond these matters. The dewatering and other mine-related water impacts were issues of contention. However, the Adani expert told the court that whatever the impacts, they 'can and will be avoided, mitigated or offset'. This covers all bases – except the possibility of failure. Under the *EPBC Act*, Adani is required to secure a minimum 90 hectares of land to offset any loss of the palms.

In the President's summing up she said 'It is clear that Waxy Cabbage Palm is a vulnerable species and that the Carmichael River population is the most significant in the world. Beyond that, little appears certain. There is uncertainty as to the optimum conditions that are necessary for the continued likely survival of the Carmichael River population. It is also uncertain what impact the mining operations will have.'

One might have thought the President would have reached a risk-averse decision, rather she concluded 'I consider that the offset and management conditions in the draft environmental authority are sufficient to avoid, mitigate or offset the potential damage to the waxy cabbage palm'.

Now it is the turn of the Black-throated Finch. The first thing to note is that the draft environmental authority and the Coordinator-General's evaluation require that certain conditions be met. Crucial to the success of the project is the provision of offsets. In association with the necessary biodiversity offset strategy there has to be a Black-throated Finch species management plan. Note in passing that the biodiversity offset plan must be 'reviewed and reported on by 5 years after the environmental authority issue and then every 5 years'. There can be no clearer statement that mining will occur. The assumption has to be that offsetting will be successful. All available evidence suggests serious doubts.

The finch management plan has to include 'a baseline research program on specific nesting and feeding requirements … a baseline research program to establish whether the [finches] at the project management site are sedentary, locally migratory or regionally migratory … a description of how the results of … research are to be used … mitigation measures to be undertaken to avoid, mitigate and manage impacts … including rehabilitation'.

We know so little! Yet, the mine has been approved.

One basic matter that the opposing scientists were able to agree on was the various possibilities for the finches as their habitat is cleared for the mine. The likely outcomes are: they will not find a suitable home and die; they will find a suitable habitat already occupied by Black-throated Finches, which cannot sustain an increased carrying capacity, resulting in further disposal or death; they will find suitable habitat that is already occupied by the same species and newcomers displace the original finches, and; they find suitable habitat not currently occupied by a resident population and it, therefore, could support the displaced finches.

The two experts agreed that if no nearby offset habitats could be found and secured, the first three scenarios were the most probable. The Adani expert agreed that the information in EIS 'could not be relied on to confidently assess the … potential impacts to the Black-throated Finch, the suitability of proposed mitigating or the appropriateness of any offsets'.

The President of the court concluded that 'there will be significant loss of Black-throated Finch with a consequential threat to the continued survival of the species in the area of the mine'. On this basis she proposed additional conditions.

In summary, it is obvious that there was far from adequate information on the range of crucial matters pertaining to the survival Black-throated Finch. It is also the case that a large amount of research will be needed before there is any certainty on the future of the finch. And then it could be that saving the species is not possible.

This brings me to the last matter I shall comment on, the economics of the mine. Here the President had real difficulty in comprehending the conflicting arguments. There is little point in repeating most of what she concluded. However, to gain an overview of the issues we find that the Queensland Coordinator-General concluded that the mine 'would deliver substantial economic benefits'. On the other hand, an economist for the objectors provided numbers which, if correct, would mean the project was unprofitable. There was no resolution of this issue.

The argument over the quantum of royalties takes us nowhere. An economist for the objectors stated: 'No witness had confidently attested to the accuracy of the royalty figures provided to the Court. For those reasons little reliance could be placed on the royalty figures provided by the applicant'. The Queensland Treasury should have been asked to present evidence as to the value of royalties it expected.

The issue of whether or not the Adani coal would compensate for increased demand in India or simply increase supply with no change in demand was another unresolved matter. The President of the court did not accept the case that there would be an uncompensated increase in supply, rather the Adani coal would be to meet increased demand or drive other coal suppliers out of the market.

She could be correct – however, no substantial evidence was presented to the court. A matter that follows from the President's proposition is that the coal from the Adani mine when burned would not lead to an increase in carbon dioxide. This reasoning is obviously wrong if there is increased demand.

There is a statement by the President which is hard to follow. She comments 'there will be no increase in Scope 3 [greenhouse gas emissions from burning coal] if the mine is not approved because other coal will be obtained from elsewhere' (p. 105). If the mine is allowed to open, or if not, and the same amount of coal is supplied in India to meet an increase in demand, there will be an increase in emissions.

I noted early that there was no cost-benefit analysis done for the EIS and its supplements. This has made the task of calculating whether or the mine is justified on economic grounds impossible, although, as noted, some have found benefits that the rest of us can't locate. Benefits were identified before the long-overdue cost-benefit analysis was submitted to the Land Court.

The results of the cost-benefit analysis where disputed in the court hearings – and are disputed to this very day. A serious lack of clarity (where did the numbers come from?) and flawed economics combined to suggest a large economic benefit. There is nothing that I can do about the veracity of the numbers without sitting down with Mr Adani and working through his business plan for the next 60 years. However, I would be surprised if this sort of exercise has not been tried by economists in the Queensland government. That the Queensland government gives support (if only lukewarm) to the mine, it must have some understanding of the expected profitability of the mine. It is on profits generated that royalties are paid to us, the owners of the coal.

It is incumbent on the Queensland government to tell us the size of the expected royalties. Likewise, the Commonwealth government must have some reasonable idea of the annual tax take from the mine and it needs to inform us of that amount. The fact that the required numbers are not on the table suggests that either the governments have failed to make head or tail of the economics of the mine, or the governments think we, the owners of the coal, don't care. There is mounting evidence that we do care.

I hesitate to conclude by discussing a flaw in the economics underpinning the Adani cost-benefit analysis, yet it is one final example of an overall flawed submission by Adani. That this has been proven to be the case is somewhat surprising – surprising in that Adani did not engage full-heartedly with its consultants and government officials; surprising that after many years of assessment, the key officials in both the Queensland and Commonwealth governments failed to obtain from Adani the evidence needed to justify the mine.

The economic flaw is easy to explain. The Adani economist presented evidence on both the 'producer surplus', roughly akin to profits, and the 'consumer surplus'. The latter is a concept that many non-economists don't readily take to. It is based on the idea that many of us would have been willing to pay more than the market price that we are required to pay for the first few items in the bundle of goods and services we purchase. Economists can calculate the total amount 'gained' by consumers in these circumstances. Adani's economist arrived at a very large consumer surplus. Now, for a consumer surplus to be recorded it would have to be India, and gained by consumers of electricity. It has nothing to do with Australian's economic well-being.

But be mindful that an increase in consumer surplus will only be generated if the extra coal sold into India is of such a large quantity that the price of coal drops in India and there is a subsequent drop in the price of electricity to Indian consumers. As the Adani mine is what economists call the 'marginal supplier', there is no expectation that there will be any decrease in electricity price. Hence, do not expect a consumer surplus. The cost-benefit analysis is wrong.

The poorest of the poor Indians will not gain anything from this mine. The middle-class Indians will not see their electricity prices drop. Mr Adani has some prospect of becoming even richer. The Queenslanders who own the coal might give it away. The Australian taxpayers might forgo some extra tax.

The Black-throated Finch might leave us for good.

Postscript

As this book went to the printer, politicians raised the spectre of 'sovereign risk' if the Commonwealth government revoked its conditional approval of the Adani mine. Sovereign risk in this case implies that the country cannot be trusted to meet its obligations to a foreign business. This is an extension of the traditional economic definition of sovereign risk. Let us not quibble about that.

However, for the record we must note that sovereign risk commonly pertains to nationalisation of property that has come to be owned by a foreign company. This is not relevant in the Adani case as the property in question is coal owned by the people of Queensland. We have not sold the coal to Adani.

What the people of Queensland have done, through the decisions of both the Queensland and Commonwealth governments, is give Adani the privilege to mine coal in a designated area, for a defined period, on the basis that Adani meets various conditions. Some of these conditions are environmental while others are economic.

Adani's right to mine is far from open-ended, rather it is a strongly stated social licence, and like any licence it can be revoked.

The Commonwealth Environment Minister's conditional approval of the mine was made under the auspices of the *Environment Protection Biodiversity Conservation Act*. Section 145 of this statute allows for an approval to be revoked if new scientific evidence is produced that, had it been known at the time of the approval being given, would have resulted in a denial to open the mine.

Much new scientific evidence was presented in the formal hearings of the Land Court of Queensland and this only became available in December 2015. Clearly, the minister, who was Greg Hunt at the time the approval was given in late July 2014, was not able to take this evidence into account. Obviously, the new Environment Minister, Josh Frydenberg, can do so. Section 145 of the *Environment Protection Biodiversity Conservation Act* was written with this express situation in mind.

It is now 2018, and the lack of action on this matter is of increasing concern.

Some of the most important conditions require Adani to successfully compensate for environmental damage that inevitably occurs from mining. Adani is to take actions that ensure that there is to be no net loss of ecological functioning and relationships. Take two examples: the Black-throated Finch population and its health and long-term survival are to be guaranteed; there is to be no loss of water to graziers and the environment.

If the evidence mounts that Adani cannot meet these and other conditions, it forfeits its privilege to mine the coal.

This is far removed from a sovereign risk situation. Many things in life, and particularly in business, are conditional on defined outcomes. This is the situation Adani is in. If it is going to mine coal at the Carmichael River site, it is in its hands to prove it can meet the imposed conditions.

The Australian public, the Queenslanders who own the coal and the farmers who are neighbours to the proposed mine, sit in judgement.

Acknowledgements

It was my lucky day when I rang Nick Walker, Director of Australian Scholarly Publishing, and said I was writing a short book on the proposed coal mine in central Queensland, a mine commonly called the Adani mine. Nick was more than happy to read of my rough draft and he came to encourage me to complete the task. When I stopped writing in early 2018, the Adani mine was a daily news topic. The story was fast moving and I discovered to my delight that Australian Scholarly Publishing was very fast in taking my draft through to publication. Thank you, Nick.

I am extremely grateful that friends and colleagues of mine made time in their busy lives to read all or parts of drafts of the book and alert me to matters deserving more clarity than I had given them. In particular I offer my thanks to lawyer friends Sean Ryan and Revel Pointon. Revel is past environmental management student of mine. My University of Queensland colleague, Dr April Reside, was my sounding board on the life of the Black-throated Finch. Sarinah Golden and Tanya Dodgen ever so willing brought fresh eyes to the topic and helped iron out some of my rough and ready writing style.

Of course, at the end of the day I remain responsible for the end product.

About the Author

Painting by Max Vosloo, 2017

Tor Hundloe is an Emeritus Professor at the University of Queensland. He was made a Member of the Order of Australia [AM] in 2003 for his contribution to: environmental economics, protected area management, coastal management, ecotourism and fisheries. Also in 2003 he was awarded a Centenary Medal for education.

In addition to a very long academic career, Tor Hundloe spent six years as the Environment Commissioner of the Industry Commission, six years as Chair of the Wet Tropics Management Authority and decades researching the human use of the Great Barrier Reef. Before he became an academic, he spent 13 years, from the age of 14, in outback shearing sheds.

Tor Hundloe is author or editor of numerous books. The three most recent: 1. the transformation of the Gold Coast from a wilderness to a 'glitter' city; 2. the future of Australian agriculture in a 'clean-green' consumer world; 3. a holistic analysis of a catchment.

Printed in Australia
AUHW020855200922
369222AU00012B/95